UNEVEN GROWT

UNEVEN GROWTH

Tactical Urbanisms for Expanding Megacities

Pedro Gadanho

The Museum of Modern Art,
New York

Published in conjunction with the exhibition
*Uneven Growth: Tactical Urbanisms for Expanding
Megacities*, at The Museum of Modern Art,
New York, November 22, 2014–May 10, 2015,
organized by Pedro Gadanho, Curator,
with Phoebe Springstubb, Curatorial Assistant,
Department of Architecture and Design.

*Uneven Growth: Tactical Urbanisms
for Expanding Megacities* is organized by
The Museum of Modern Art, New York, in
collaboration with MAK – Austrian Museum
of Applied Arts / Contemporary Art, Vienna.

This is the third exhibition in the series Issues
in Contemporary Architecture, supported by
Andre Singer.

The exhibition and accompanying workshop
at MoMA PS1 were made possible by MoMA's
Wallis Annenberg Fund for Innovation in
Contemporary Art through the Annenberg
Foundation.

Major support is provided by The International
Council of The Museum of Modern Art.

Additional funding is provided by the
MoMA Annual Exhibition Fund.

Support for this publication is provided
by the Dale S. and Norman Mills Leff
Publication Fund.

Produced by the Department of Publications,
The Museum of Modern Art, New York

Edited by Ron Broadhurst
Designed by Project Projects
Production by Hannah Kim
Printed and bound by
Ofset Yapimevi, Istanbul

This book is typeset in Marr Sans and
Besley 2-line Grotesque Outline.
The paper is 120 gsm Alkim uncoated.

Library of Congress Control Number:
2014949058
ISBN: 978-0-87070-914-2

Published by
The Museum of Modern Art
11 West 53 Street, New York,
New York 10019
www.moma.org

Distributed in the
United States and Canada
by ARTBOOK | D.A.P., New York

155 Sixth Avenue, 2nd floor,
New York, New York 10013
www.artbook.com

Distributed outside the
United States and Canada
by Thames & Hudson Ltd

181A High Holborn,
London WC1V 7QX
www.thamesandhudson.com

Cover and back cover: Tuca Vieira.
*Paraisópolis favela bordering
the affluent district of Morumbi,
São Paulo.* 2008

Printed in Turkey

DESIGN SCENARIOS AND
TACTICAL URBANISMS

Foreword

It is now fifty years since Bernard Rudofsky's influential exhibition *Architecture without Architects* opened at The Museum of Modern Art. Featuring photographs of vernacular architecture from Machu Picchu to the nomadic structures of the Atlas Mountains in an immersive installation, Rudofsky proposed "to break down our narrow concepts of the art of building by introducing the unfamiliar world of nonpedigreed architecture." Bringing to light a genre rarely considered within the Museum's walls, the exhibition disavowed the usual architect-protagonists to reflect on semivernacular, communal contexts of architectural production as provocation to architectural modernism. With *Uneven Growth*, the third exhibition in the series Issues in Contemporary Architecture, curator Pedro Gadanho revives and expands Rudofsky's link between popular "homegrown" architectures of necessity and architecture with a capital *A* to include a new "informal" urban setting in which, again, large areas of the built environment are not made by architects. In the face of the United Nations's rising World Urbanization Prospects and, closer to home, the income inequality and housing crisis of the city just beyond the Museum's doors, *Uneven Growth*, like *Architecture without Architects* before it, seeks unexpected sources of inspiration and offers a fresh look at the means and methods by which the urban environment is constructed.

The six speculative proposals presented in this catalogue are the result of a productive and dynamic fourteen-month initiative spanning multiple continents and bringing together architects of local knowledge and international experience. Keenly observed and city-specific—from the *varanda* culture of Rio de Janeiro to the water-centric habitats of Lagos—the proposals represent an experiment in new, outside-the-box working methods that turn on interdisciplinary knowledge. Paired with essays by a group of curators, scholars, and critics that situate the megacity against broader socio-political and global conditions, the proposals of this volume offer both a much-needed resource and a conversation-starter for the active engagement of the public, designers, urbanists, students, and city officials with their cities.

I congratulate curator Pedro Gadanho for his dedication and insightful organization of this catalogue and exhibition. My sincere thanks go to the MAK - Austrian Museum of Applied Arts / Contemporary Art and its Director, Christoph Thun-Hohenstein, who have been both generous hosts—organizing the project's final workshop and providing a second venue for the exhibition at its 2015 Vienna Biennale—and consummate collaborators in the project's formation. On behalf of the Trustees and the staff of the Museum, I would like to thank Andre Singer for his generous support of the exhibition, the third in the series Issues in Contemporary Architecture that he has supported. In addition, for their support of the exhibition and the accompanying workshop at MoMA PS1, I am grateful to MoMA's Wallis Annenberg Fund for Innovation in Contemporary Art through the Annenberg Foundation; to the MoMA Annual Exhibition Fund; and to the Dale S. and Norman Mills Leff Publication Fund for its support of this book.

—Glenn D. Lowry
Director, The Museum of Modern Art

Foreword

By traditional definition architects are not social workers. And yet even in the distant past they were supposed to contribute with their ideas and projects to society at large. Built architecture is always a mirror of the "state of civilization" of a particular place and time, irrespective of the nature of the building and its financial underpinning. In our century, it has become abundantly clear that architects will have to be first and foremost social workers if the profession is to retain its relevance and go beyond the "architecture-as-art" glamour projects that some cities and countries still rely on to impress the world.

This is all the more important as we live in a new modernity, which I tend to call "digital modernity." While the previous Western modernity—to which Vienna around 1900 was a major interdisciplinary contributor—had to come to grips with, and use the potential of, industrialization, our new modernity has to deal with the fundamental implications of the digitalization of our world. A truly global phenomenon, digital modernity has the potential to bring forth positive change, be it by using communication design to substantially reduce our ecological footprint or by kickstarting innovative architectural processes.

To shoulder the task of designing open systems, architecture needs to take an interdisciplinary approach. Younger generations of architects are bringing a fresh sense of "holistic responsibility" to the discipline, relying less on the notion of architecture as a total work of art (*Gesamtkunstwerk*) and instead sharing the responsibility with users to breathe life into built structures. Today's architecture has to become more flexible and dynamic, leaving space for development beyond the original design intentions. It is even imaginable that the concept of the *Gesamtkunstwerk* will turn into something entirely new, a widely shared understanding that the very core of an architectural project is its "irresistibly responsible" use, a crowdsourcing of sorts. What sounds like abandoning control—always difficult for architects—in reality results in retaining it by creating an intelligent margin for manoeuvering in which people can use the structures as designed.

Against this background, I am particularly happy with *Uneven Growth: Tactical Urbanisms for Expanding Megacities*. The Museum of Modern Art, New York, has been at the forefront of international developments in architecture for almost nine decades and, more recently—starting with Andres Lepik's already legendary exhibition at MoMA, *Small Scale, Big Change*—led the way in opening the world's eyes to the potential of architecture for positive change. Pedro Gadanho brings fresh insights to the topic. For the MAK – Austrian Museum of Applied Arts / Contemporary Art, in Vienna, which while celebrating its 150th anniversary made positive change its key focus, it was logical to invite Gadanho to become architecture curator of the Vienna Biennale in 2015. This invitation quickly turned into a collaboration between two of the most important truly multidisciplinary museums today to produce an exhibition on the role of architecture in the future of megacities, to be shown in New York and Vienna.

I would like to thank MoMA Director Glenn Lowry and Barry Bergdoll, MoMA's Curator, Department of Architecture and Design, for making this exciting collaboration possible. My special thanks go to Gadanho and the six participating design teams as well as all others at MoMA and MAK working on the project. May it contribute to improving the world!

—Christoph Thun-Hohenstein
Director, MAK - Austrian Museum of Applied Arts / Contemporary Art

Preface

The Museum of Modern Art is a laboratory: in its experiments the public is invited to participate.
—Alfred H. Barr, Jr., in *Art in Our Time*, 1939[1]

From its founding, the Department of Architecture and Design has been associated not only with recording the changing face of architecture and the expanded capacity of the architectural profession, but also advocating for change. In the inaugural show, which coined the term "International Style," Henry-Russell Hitchcock and Philip Johnson, along with Alfred Barr, set out to direct American architecture, not the least in a section developed by Lewis Mumford on the housing crisis of the early years of the Great Depression. In the late 1960s and 1970s again the museum experimented overtly with the laboratory metaphor, notably in 1967 inviting a set of university-led teams of architects to consider urban solutions that could be alternatives to the then reigning doctrine of urban renewal. Four areas of Manhattan and the nearby Bronx were chosen as test cases for working with existing fabric rather than wholesale bulldozing to provide a new way of looking, making, and thinking about the city, the results displayed in 1967 as *The New City*.

Initiated in 2009, the Issues in Contemporary Architecture series aims to revive that lapsed legacy, and to find again innovative ways for a museum to engage with some of the most pressing issues facing society today. The goal is to make manifest that the design professions have much to offer at the first stages of framing issues rather than only late in the game once other modes of thinking and planning have worked through a set of problems. In contrast with the more normative demeanor of exhibiting architectural practice, this is an activist curatorial mode, one that complements what I have elsewhere labeled the reactive mode of exhibition.[2] In such a mode, rather than waiting for others to take the lead, the museum instigates and takes risks, setting problems that the status quo or the marketplace do not formulate, committing to showing experimental results that do not yet exist. *Rising Currents: Projects for New York's Waterfront* was the first workshop/exhibition in that laboratorial series, of which *Uneven Growth*, presented here, is now the third iteration.[3]

With *Rising Currents*, the museum served in an all but unprecedented way as the incubator rather than the mirror of new ideas. These ideas were intended not only for instigating a debate on New York City's relationship to the sea level rise—something made potently evident almost two years to the day after the show's closing when Superstorm Sandy struck the region—but also to provide ideas and images that might help activate the debate for the millions and millions of people worldwide living in floodable zones. *Rising Currents* was the result of a three-month-long workshop held at a studio space at MoMA PS1, in which teams assembled for interdisciplinary collaborations alternating long hours of teamwork with critiques by invited experts in a range of disciplines from hydraulics to public transportation.

Two years later, in *Foreclosed: Rehousing the American Dream* (2012), the same approach was staged to address the challenges of the urban fringe of five American cities hard hit by the subprime mortgage crisis and the tsunami of foreclosures that came in its wake. Again interdisciplinary teams were tasked with thinking about an urbanization of older suburbs that might ameliorate specific places and reopen the debate on the place of housing and transportation in the privatized development economy of the United States. Borrowing a line from Chicago mayor Rahm Emmanuel, then White House chief of staff, it was important for the design culture of the museum never to let a good crisis go to waste.[4]

For the third edition in the series, Pedro Gadanho has turned to a crisis every bit as global, threatening, and daunting as rising sea levels, namely accelerated income discrepancy, a polarization of wealth and poverty that can be read in various ways in our rapidly urbanizing planet. By now everyone knows that a threshold was reached a few years ago when the UN reported than for the first time in recorded history more than half the world's population lives in cities. By the mid-twenty-first century, a more recent UN report suggests, the urban population will swell to 67 percent of the world's population. As a recent report in *The Economist* notes, that means that "for the next 36 years the world's cities will expand by the equivalent of six São Paulos every year."[5] The last forty years too have seen a dramatic increase in what have come to be called the "informal city," a term intended to replace the negative connotations both of slums and of a centralized government-sponsored urban renewal often known as "slum clearance," with a valorizing frame of reference. In the face of this, inaction is not an option. With estimates that by 2030 some two billion people, or nearly a quarter of humanity, will be living in illegal dwellings,[6] the tactics for confronting the rising tide of the informal city is one of the most pressing and perplexing issues facing the planet.

Uneven Growth is a laboratory experiment devoted to the pressing issue not only of ameliorating life in the expanding informal city but—as in *Foreclosed*—to defining an effective and activist role for architects in the wake of two generations of disinvestment in public projects from housing to urban infrastructure. In recent years, a growing number of younger architects and designers have begun to act on the commitment to the idea that the informal settlement, or favela—borrowing the word coined many decades ago for the slums

of Rio de Janeiro—are here to stay and require selective intervention rather than wholesale demolition so as to achieve better daily living and enhanced community ties. With their actions they have attempted to redress the results—if not the causes—of the ever-widening chasm in the distribution of wealth and access to services.

Tactical urbanism, a term that covers many of these practices, is a highly pragmatic movement that abandons all holistic and comprehensive planning as either failed in its historical record or doomed by the worldwide ascent of neo-liberal economy and politics. It is, however, an elastic movement in that it applies to a spectrum of designers, from those who perform guerrilla intervention of short-term change, often equivalent to the illegal settlements that are at the birth of many urban favelas, to those who seek to prod, provoke, or stimulate the political process toward incremental realization of fragments of what might be larger networks. Such, for instance, are the infrastructure projects of a group like Urban-Think Tank, whose fragment of a cable car extension to Caracas's public transportation system to weave dense informal quarters into the larger network of the Venezuelan capital was featured in MoMA's 2010 exhibition *Small Scale, Big Change: New Architectures of Social Engagement*.

This is a growing trend, in which local knowledge and global expertise

might be combined. The novelty of the workshop framed by Pedro Gadanho resides precisely in this notion. As in previous iterations of the series, the results are brimming with fresh ideas, striking imaging and imagining, and approaches that are at once specific and adaptable. The enterprise, like tactical urbanism in general, is not free of paradoxes. It seems, for instance, hard to reconcile the gap between the modest scale of some interventions and the dimensions of the worldwide urban and economic crisis that so urgently needs to be addressed. But even as faith in systems, in blueprints, and in master plans has completely collapsed, the optimism of the projects developed here is best embodied in those that want to create paradigms, exemplars, open-ended interventions, and other actions that have at their heart the hopes of a multiplier effect. Strikingly many of the projects take to the roofscape to develop new spaces, new interactions, and new realms for a public zone in situations of dense family occupation. Alternative models not only of building but of ownership and cooperation among citizens are proposed as an invitation to think alternatively rather than as a set of blueprints; some can be realized ad hoc, others presuppose alterations to existing systems at a larger level of the financial, municipal administrative, or legal regimes.

It remains to be seen if the individual achievements of tactical urbanism's incarnations—of which there are more every month—can aggregate into an ever-larger impact. However, with *Uneven Growth*'s invitation to deploy such mode of operation in some of the most rapidly growing urban situations across the planet, a rich array of ideas, images, and new thinking and hopefulness has already been reaped.

—Barry Bergdoll
Curator, Department of Architecture and Design, The Museum of Modern Art

1   Barr, MoMA's founding director, was writing in the catalogue of the Museum's tenth anniversary exhibition.

2   Barry Bergdoll, "The Art of Advocacy: The Museum as Design Laboratory," *Design Observer*, September 16, 2011. The reactive mode, adapted from the practice of art curation, is one where the architecture curator culls from contemporary or recent production what he or she admires and thinks deserves contextualization and publicity. Such exhibitions have had enormous impact, from MoMA's inaugural show of 1932, with its promulgation of the International Style, to *Deconstructivist Architecture* of 1988.

3   See Barry Bergdoll, *Rising Currents: Projects for New York's Waterfront* (New York: Museum of Modern Art, 2010).

4   See Barry Bergdoll and Reinhold Martin, *Foreclosed: Rehousing the American Dream* (New York: The Museum of Modern Art, 2012).

5   "Urbanisation: Roads of Redemption," *The Economist*, June 21, 2014, 59.

6   Cited in Justin McGuirk, *Radical Cities: Across Latin America in Search of a New Architecture* (London and New York: Verso, 2014), 109.

MIRRORING UNEVEN GROWTH

A Speculation on Tomorrow's Cities Today

Pedro Gadanho

The design scenarios in *Uneven Growth* presuppose that the anticipation of impending, plausible urban visions may prompt a critical understanding of present problems—thus contributing to fuel the public debate on the same issues.

Sze Tsung Leong. *Nan Shi, Huangpu District, Shanghai.* 2004. Chromogenic color print, 31⅞ × 40⅛" (81 × 101.8 cm). The Museum of Modern Art, New York. Fund for the Twenty-First Century

As urbanization continues to expand across the globe, the distribution of spatial and economic resources in cities is increasingly lopsided. As evidenced by numerous academic studies, inequality is growing. In spite of the promise of amelioration that urban migration once represented, life conditions deteriorate for large segments of expanding urban populations. Simultaneously, traditional, centralized urban planning seems to fail when faced with the rising presence of informal settlements, gentrification processes, and other urban phenomena of our days. Driven by ideology or economic incapacity, the ability of the national state to intervene in the contemporary city seems to recede everywhere.

As problematic urban conditions progressively become a subject of concern for specialists in various fields, cities also continue to be the most important sites for everyday struggles at the levels of political governance, civil rights, and social protest. Urban dwellers' claims for spatial justice and the right to the city appear in multiple forms of appropriation—from the Occupy movement to the Arab Spring, but also in the guise of do-it-yourself urbanism, bottom-up attempts at community self-management, and other tactical forms of urban intervention.

Despite the technological optimism that surrounds some recent urban developments—with its promises of smart management systems, utter social connectivity, and apps for every possible need—large cities around the world are also hotbeds of conceivable catastrophe. Within a gradually globalized order, megacities, megalopolises, and other large urban networks are crucial nodes for flows of information and people. Accordingly, they also contain the potential to rapidly propagate any crisis or collapse to the whole system.

As large cities can no longer be seen as isolated, self-sufficient entities, their current and oncoming problems may be anticipated to bear massive impact at a global level.

With the planet facing dwindling resources, climate change, and other instabilities, the potential for human catastrophe contained in current urban development has been a regular subject of scholarly research. For sure, city authorities, urban thinkers, economists, and other world protagonists are already joining forces to understand and tackle this issue, having to ensure that over the next decades a constantly expanding urban realm will remain habitable, sustainable, and resilient.

Despite the urgency of these matters, despite the many initiatives that over the last years have sought to bring these problems to light, still the imbalanced growth of the contemporary urban realm is failing to trigger a broader public debate. This alone would make it reason enough for The Museum of Modern Art to join the ongoing efforts to address these problems in academia, in coalitions of cities, and in other international forums. Global museums no longer being exclusively seen as repositories of art, they may take advantage of their public visibility to assume a specific role in promoting awareness, cultural activism, and intellectual discussion at a wider scale.

Assuming the need to expand the responsibility of leading art institutions to new understandings of culture, it was decided that the third iteration of MoMA's Issues In Contemporary Architecture series should adhere to the international debate on the future of major cities, in collaboration with the MAK - Museum of Applied Arts / Contemporary Art, in Vienna. Following previous initiatives by MoMA's Architecture and Design

Department that had engaged interdisciplinary design teams to tackle the effects of rising sea levels in New York, or the impact of the foreclosure crisis in the United States, *Uneven Growth: Tactical Urbanisms for Expanding Megacities* brings together six "collaboratives" of local practitioners and international researchers to examine new design possibilities for six global metropolises: Hong Kong, Istanbul, Lagos, Mumbai, New York, and Rio de Janeiro.

26'10 south Architects. Taxi Rank No. 2, Diepsloot, South Africa. 2008–11

As in previous instances, the curatorial process relied on the creation of unprecedented design proposals through the articulation of public workshops, an exhibition, and this publication. Given the transnational nature of the design teams invited to participate in the project, workshops were held in different venues around the globe, in New York, in Shenzhen, and in Vienna, over the course of one year of brainstorming and discussion. As part of their brief, participants were asked to come up with *design scenarios*, i.e., design solutions for future developments, which would simultaneously raise awareness of the prevailing inequalities in specific urban contexts and confront the changing roles of architects and urban designers vis-à-vis the evolution of cities.

At the heart of the project lies the optimistic belief that current design thinking can effectively contribute to the current urban debate. Early modern architects and urban designers were recognized for the sense of social responsibility to which they adhered in their the efforts of modernization and urbanization at the dawn of the twentieth century. The twenty-first century, however, presents us with new and overwhelming challenges in the urban realm. As such, it is urgent that, after much data has been collected on the uneven urban developments of the last years, architects and designers again attempt to address the urban problem with responsible, if tentative, propositions. In contrast to other forms of urban speculation, it is imperative that designers' visions for the future are deployed as a critical tool to reflect upon the problems of today.

1. State of the City

> In 2008, the world reaches an invisible but momentous milestone: for the first time in history, more than half its human population, 3.3 billion people, will be living in urban areas. By 2030, this is expected to swell to almost five billion. Many of the new urbanites will be poor. Their future, the future of cities in developing countries, the future of humanity itself, all depend very much on decisions made now in preparation for this growth.
> —City Mayors Society

In 2030, the world's population will be a staggering eight billion people. Of these, two-thirds will live in cities. Most will be poor. With limited resources this profoundly unbalanced growth will be one of the greatest challenges to be faced by societies ever more connected across the globe.

Contrary to popular belief and as experts have demonstrated, urban imbalances have been on the rise over the last three decades. Income disparity, socioeconomic divisions, and spatial inequalities have sharply increased in the most advanced world cities and in emergent megalopolises alike. As sociologist Saskia Sassen has pointed out, the time is long gone when manufacturing in and around cities "created the conditions for the expansion of a vast middle class."[1] Today, the escalation of the financial services industry in major cities has instead driven up the incomes of the top percentiles of urban populations while it has reduced the "real earnings of workers with the least education."

And while rural populations are still migrating to urban conglomerations and contributing to the growth of megalopolises around the globe, their drive no longer lies in the mirage of equal employment opportunities. As Mike Davis has noted in *Planet of Slums*, rural dwellers are rather pushed to cities—and more precisely to their expanding informal districts—because of a global deterioration of rural conditions.[2] As a consequence of rural-urban migration, urban poverty is on the rise. Due to decreasing upward social mobility and degradation of the lower middle classes, poorer populations in the bigger cities are progressively marginalized into "poverty regimes" that seem more and more to be inescapable.[3]

Even if contemporary cities rely heavily on the services of low-wage workers to sustain their economies, they lack the capacity to absorb the fast-growing numbers of new urban dwellers into their existing formal structure. Thus, informal urbanization expands and, in more or less visible fashion, furthers existing spatial and social segregations.[4] Often, the resulting urban slums develop their own productive structures, but their populations are nonetheless trapped in a state of chronic poverty: they are blighted by inadequate shelter and health conditions, divested of adequate means to improve their circumstances, and also often deprived of any political and civic rights.

The explosive urban condition sketched here reveals slight variations around the globe. While it may differ according to diverse states of development, it leads to the same question: How can these forms of social and spatial segregation be addressed? As specialists, benefactors, and institutions such as the World Bank struggle to define the policies and economical mechanisms that may contribute to any kind of improvement, is it even conceivable that such afflictions can be addressed from a design point of view? Can design thinking engage with policy makers and participative community

forums,[5] as well as the latest technological leaps, so as to provide empowerment to urban dwellers who have been dispossessed of practically every resource and right?

This is the challenge that *Uneven Growth* presented to architects and urban designers practicing in local and international contexts. Teaming up with their respective research and design skills, they were prompted to contribute with critical reflection and a robust vision for how these problems are to be faced in different yet not completely dissimilar urban contexts. In the face of a chosen urban study case, each "collaborative" was asked to turn the potential for catastrophe on its head and explore how the state of urban emergency suggested here is to fuel new modes of design creativity.

With the majority of the planet's population transitioning to urban environments, and with the problems that arise from a diffuse, uneven

urban condition, much attention has been dedicated to large urban structures in the form of books, exhibitions, and academic research. Concerns over the current city— and, in many cases, over the emergence of informal, so-called "shadow cities"[6]—became widely shared in experts' circles, and have prompted cultural institutions, professional bodies, governments, and gurus alike to discuss an increasingly daunting urban condition.[7]

To name only a few of the cultural endeavors dedicated to urban phenomena in the last fifteen years, the exhibition *Century City* was mounted in 2001 at the Tate Modern in London; *Mutations* was presented during the same year at the Arc en Rêve Centre d'Architecture in Bordeaux; and, under the direction of Ricky Burdett, the Architecture Biennale in Venice was entirely dedicated to the subject in 2006. These were large exhibitions presenting overwhelming analyses

"A cidade é nossa, ocupe-a" (The city is ours, occupy it). Avenida conde da Boa Vista in Recife, Brazil. 2013

Urban-Think Tank. Metro Cable, San Agustin, Caracas. 2007–10

and data on current problems in and cultural production out of global urban agglomerations.

Other urban researchers, as well as architects such as Rem Koolhaas, have undertaken countless studies on the nature and phenomena of exploding urban areas, namely in China, Latin America, and Africa. And more recently, while numerous agencies and organizations turned to urban issues, museums and universities joined efforts with global corporations to investigate specific urban transformations. Such was the case of the BMW Guggenheim Lab, launched in 2011, and the Audi Urban Future Initiative, hosted by Columbia University in 2013, to mention just two New York–based initiatives dedicated to the theme of future urban mobility.

Vis-à-vis such intense production of knowledge on urban development, *Uneven Growth* was always intended as a next step. Taking advantage of a museum platform with global reach, the project is intended to bring these topics to a wider and more mixed international audience, fostering a public debate beyond specialized

discourse. Simultaneously, it seeks to present design proposals that reflect the urban conditions of different world regions, but also to disclose changing design attitudes toward unequal urban contexts.

2. Tactical Urbanisms and Changing Architectural Practices

A practice of the order constructed by others redistributes its space; it creates at least a certain play in that order, a space for maneuvers of unequal forces and for utopian points of reference. [Innumerable ways of playing with] the space instituted by others characterize the subtle, stubborn resistant activity of groups which, since they lack their own space, have to get along in a network of already established forms and representations.
—Michel de Certeau, *The Practice of Everyday Life*[8]

Urban agglomeration continues to be seen as a sustainable form of human settlement, especially when faced with an inevitable dwindling of

natural resources.[9] Yet, as we have briefly analyzed, social conditions in megacities deteriorate, inequality grows, and top-down urban planning fails when confronted with rising informality.

Contrary to state initiatives that during most of the twentieth century provided Western nations with heavy investment in mass dwelling and urban infrastructures, in developing countries today city and state authorities remain unable to confront the pace and extension of informal conglomeration in and around major cities.

In a not too distant past, industrialization and social motivations allowed the nation-state to tackle economic disparities within European and North American metropolises. Today, however, slum eradication in megacities with a global presence takes place only where market forces drive social displacement in the name of land value and gentrification. Similarly, as much as architects and urban planners have played a crucial role in addressing the need for affordable housing and an operative city, today they too seem impotent considering the speed at which radical urban inequalities settle in place.

Although attempts are still being made at municipal and regional planning, top-down action, particularly in developing megacities, is mostly entangled in inefficient politics, corrupt bureaucracy, and economic insufficiency.[10] Moreover, with a general turn to neo-liberal policies around the globe—coincident with cyclic financial crises, slowing economic growth, and the constantly impending collapse of any kind of welfare system—top-down urban management recedes even in the most advanced and stable urban centers. While mayors and municipal authorities have taken the lead in raising the profile of their cities in a competitive international panorama, urban inequities still flourish and discontent eventually reaches the streets. As a reaction, if not anticipation to some of these developments, tactical forms of urbanism carried out by varied urban actors have emerged as an attempt to take urban matters into their own hands.

As a counterpart to a classic, strategic notion of top-down planning, tactical modes of urbanism have arisen in the form of everyday, bottom-up approaches to local problems within unevenly managed contemporary metropolises. With a pure notion of "tactical urbanism" made difficult by the complexities of any consequent urban project, a plurality of interpretations and embodiments of this idea have emerged to respond to the failures of an urban planning exclusively imposed from above.

Tactical urbanisms may impulsively arise from the streets, but they also emerge from given creative practices and given domains of specialization. Spontaneous takes on the spatial reinvention and appropriation of existing urban environments have thus come to combine top-down initiatives with bottom-up ingenuity, with different degrees of mutual contamination. In the form of do-it-yourself actions, hands-on-urbanism and participative urban interventions,[11] artists, architects, designers, city authorities, community leaders, and even policy makers have progressively allied with communities and local populations to produce acupunctural interventions in difficult, often unattended urban contexts. Rather than large-scale transformations unable to effectively cope with the dynamics of current urban developments, smaller, but still impactful, "urban catalysts" have pervasively become a preferred, if crossbred, mode of city intervention.[12] Even if architects and city authorities were the instigators of referential case studies of tactical urbanism—such as the unexpected installation of cable cars in the slums of Caracas—still these responded in innovative tactical fashion to pressing bottom-up needs.

Against this background, a multifaceted, hybrid notion of "tactical urbanisms" is seen here as drawing on the ideas of the late French anthropologist Michel de Certeau, who suggested that urban dwellers engage in tactical actions when they appropriate urban space on a daily basis.[13] This offers a direct if sometimes unrevealed response to the strategies imposed on them by city planners and decision makers. As de Certeau puts it, the "rationalized, expansionist and at the same time centralized, clamorous and spectacular production" of the formal city is thus counteracted by "*another production*."[14] This "other production" is precisely what emerges in today's "tactical urbanisms": a creative and resourceful appropriation of the contemporary city's conflictual conditions, expressed in terms of informal urban objects, adaptive habitat, alternative forms of infrastructure, temporary and illegal uses of public space, and vehement claims to the "right to the city."

While contributing to map these emergent modes of tactical urbanism around the globe, the *Uneven Growth* project asks precisely how current practices of architecture and urban design can learn from such developments. While compiling some examples—presented within these pages as a sample of a broader online charting open to public participation— the curatorial

intent did not, however, reside in the emulation of current forms of tactical urbanism. Rather, it proposed to understand how such practices are effectively altering the perception of the roles of architects, artists, and other urban practitioners in the face of a changing urban reality.

Most of the teams invited to participate in *Uneven Growth* had already previously revealed a changing notion of architectural practice, vis-à-vis the urban contexts in which they choose to act. Rather than serving the wealthier percentile of available private or public clients—in which much of traditional architecture takes refuge—their work often discloses how, when faced with radical city transformation, the urban designer must become an activist.[15] Further to their participation in the *Uneven Growth* project, they were invited to reflect on how tactical attitudes could inform design visions for the outcomes of contemporary urban inequality. Ultimately, this would constitute the essential drive for the creation of the exhibition's content.

Uneven Growth's curatorial project relies on the idea that tactical urbanisms provide inspiration for design tools that effectively mix top-down and bottom-up impulses.[16] Such an idea echoes what has been increasingly described as an *open-source urbanism*. While proposals for future "intelligent cities" raise eyebrows,[17] Saskia Sassen suggests that "multiple small interventions may not look like much, but together they give added meaning to the notion of the incompleteness of cities."[18] Responding tactically to this *incompleteness*— or, as others have suggested, to the city's untapped

Atelier OPA. Cardboard Shelter 1, Tokyo. 2011

Michael Wolf. *Architecture of Density #12*. 2003. C-print, 40 × 58" (101.6 × 147.3 cm). Collection the artist

resources[19]— an open-source, "hand-made urbanism"[20] may precisely mean that, as Sassen has it, cities will continue to enjoy "their long life."

3. Six Cities, Six Collaboratives

You put together two things that have not been put together before. And the world is changed. People may not notice at the time, but that doesn't matter. The world has been changed nonetheless.
—Julian Barnes, *Levels of Life*[21]

If one wants to conceive design scenarios in which tactical modes of urbanism come together to react on contemporary urban contexts, one needs to engage in concrete situations. If one wants to offer consequent, though perhaps site-specific, design visions for the future of the city, one needs to contemplate the diversity of the current urban condition. This implies that, contrary to previous editions in the Issues in Contemporary Architecture exhibition series, *Uneven Growth* should bear a global ambition. The juxtaposition of distinctive, yet comparable global megacities was essential to the curatorial endeavor.

Six megacities in six diverse world regions were selected as case studies. The choice of these urban conglomerations was essentially determined by the ways in which they display different degrees, stages, and conditions of urban inequality.

While each city generally represents the level of development of a given region, similar situations were avoided. MoMA's home city, for example, stands as a case that bears comparison to relevant but absent metropolises such as London, Paris, Tokyo, or Los Angeles. While to some New York came as an unexpected example of inequity, research—not to mention the subsequent political debate of "two cities"—would soon reveal that the financial capital of North America represented only the most advanced stages of a common, if sometimes less visible, story in urban unevenness.

The cities in *Uneven Growth* were selected on the basis of their considerable size and their potential to generate encounters between a

Iwan Baan. Makoko, Lagos. 2013. Digital photograph. Collection the artist

given cosmopolitanism and emergent modes of informal appropriation. Still, there was a clear intention to circumvent megacities that had been overexposed in research projects produced during recent years. In this circumstance, cities such as São Paulo or Mexico City were sidestepped to the advantage of another Latin American city, one that has brought the clash between planned city and informal settlement to the very core of the urban ensemble. Currently undergoing profound transformations due to global events such as the 2014 World Cup and the 2016 Olympics, Rio de Janeiro presented itself not only at the crucial intersection of future change and deeply imbedded spatial conflicts, but also at the forefront of practices of slum regeneration.[22]

The existence of urban conflicts in more or less apparent form, along with a tendency to display borders and contrasts between two worlds, were also important criteria to chose the cities that would be the focus of research. Istanbul and Hong Kong are, in their own ways, essential connectors in the increasingly important global fluxes between East and West.[23] Together with Moscow, Istanbul is the only European megacity that is still developing at a furious pace, and it was recently one of two major epicenters of violent urban protests worldwide—the other being Rio de Janeiro.[24] And while Hong Kong is also known for its protest culture, as a borderline island between China and the rest of the world it is also representative of a unique, futuristic condition of urban density.[25]

Finally, Mumbai and Lagos are notoriously relevant when it comes to exemplify the most extreme urban disparities in developing megacities around the world. With both experiencing a relatively recent but explosive population growth,[26] they are paradigmatic of situations in which urban slums assume alarming proportions,[27] alongside immense mobility issues, public health crises, and general infrastructural needs.

Faced with the scope of problems presented by each of these specific urban conditions, it soon became evident that *Uneven Growth* participants should have an intimate knowledge of local circumstances, and should be already imbedded in their object of study. Their previous practices should be somehow be entangled with their city's realities while revealing changing stances toward the potential role of architects as urban catalysts and activists. From the participative work of Mumbai-based Urbz with Dharavi's slum dwellers to NLÈ's self-initiated, semi-illegal school project in the floating shantytowns of Lagos, from MAP Office's long-standing research into the tactical nature of Hong Kong's everyday uses to Superpool, Rua Arquitetos, and SITU Studio's reflections on how new design approaches may interfere with the changing urban contexts of Istanbul, Rio, or New York, these were all teams that combined political positions with audacious design capabilities.

Rather than only commissioning these teams to come up with proposals for their respective cities, though, it was also considered that their privileged viewpoints could benefit from confrontation with other external perspectives. Given the global dimension of the contemporary urban issues explored here, collaborations of a transgeographical nature seemed to be adequate for the project's goals. As I had proposed in previous stances, in dealing with such new realities one should overcome postcolonial dichotomies and indeed promote the crossbreeding of multiple knowledges and differentiated standpoints.[28]

As such, teams involved in urban studies at an international level, even if in very different contexts, were also challenged to unite their specific research approaches to the skill sets of the designated local architectural practices. The Network Architecture Lab, at Columbia

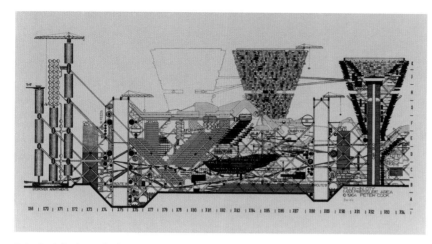

Peter Cook (Archigram). Plug-In City: Maximum Pressure Area. Project, 1962–64. Section, 1964. Ink and gouache on photomechanical print, 32⅞ × 57¹¹/₁₆" (83.5 × 146.5 cm). The Museum of Modern Art, New York. Gift of The Howard Gilman Foundation

University, Ensamble Studio's POPlab, at the Massachusetts Institute of Technology, and the master's program for Advanced Studies in Urban Design, at ETH Zurich, all represented current university-based units dedicated to urban inquiry, either looking at future applications of architectural thinking, or, in the latter case, instigating design collaborations with the developing world. On the other hand, Atelier d'Architecture Autogérée, in Paris, Inteligencias Colectivas, in Madrid, and Cohabitation Strategies, operating from Rotterdam and New York, embodied independent practices that have adopted radical new approaches to tactical urbanism and bottom-up urban prototyping as well as a political understanding of the urban habitat.

By matching these diverse design approaches into new "collaboratives," the curatorial aim of *Uneven Growth* resided in the possibility that, besides the eventual "productive conflict" of any imposed collaboration, a design chemistry could emerge that responded adequately to the complexities of the themes described here.

4. Curating Design Scenarios

It's all over the place, just termite mounds of poorly organized and extremely potent knowledge, quantifiable, interchangeable data with newly networked relations. We cannot get rid of this stuff. It is our new burden, it is there as a fact on the ground, it is a fait accompli. There are new asynchronous communication forms that are globalized and offshored, and there is the loss of a canon and a record. There is no single authoritative voice of history … This really changes the narrative, and the organized presentations of history in a way that history cannot recover from.
—Bruce Sterling, *Atemporality for the Creative Artist*[29]

Making sense of the complexities involved in today's uneven urban developments is, in itself, a highly problematic task. In the wake of proliferating tactical urbanisms, the loss of "canon" and of "a single authoritative voice" in urban planning may well be embraced as a positive aspect. Nonetheless, this leaves us with an added difficulty when it comes to construct a clear vision for the upcoming city. In fact, it may be the case that such a cohesive foresight is now impossible. We may be destined to ascertain only a fragmentary, kaleidoscopic collection of cautionary scenarios. In response to this condition, curating architecture is nowadays conceivable as a practice of establishing unforeseen juxtapositions, if not instigating creative combinations of ideas that are destined to arouse a critical awareness of current issues.

It has not always been like this, of course. A more traditional view of curating implies only a rather conservative take on the preservation and display of collectible objects. However, with the notion that curating can itself be a critical practice, this activity may have a more palpable impact in the public perception of budding collective concerns. Through new connections that are produced out of a collection, for example, or through the association of themes and experiences that have not been yet considered together, juxtaposition allows for new insights. It allows for new critical perspectives to emerge.

In the case of *Uneven Growth*, the pairing of local practices to international research teams was deemed essential to produce unforeseen perspectives on urban inequality in contemporary global cities. Additionally, the adoption of the nascent idea of "design scenarios" was also deemed essential to tackle this urban problem.

Following a method of scenario planning developed by military intelligence in the 1950s,[30] the concept of design scenarios was conceived here as combining both a technique to describe a potential future and the design approach that can be imagined in response to such depiction. Acknowledging the role that fictional techniques are increasingly playing

Superstudio. Twelve Ideal Cities: The First City. Project, 1971. Aerial Perspective. Photolithograph, 27¾ × 39⁹⁄₁₆" (70.2 × 100.6 cm). The Museum of Modern Art, New York. Given Anonymously

in architectural and design thinking,[31] the use of design scenarios in a curatorial context such as that of *Uneven Growth* presupposes that the anticipation of impending, plausible urban visions may prompt a critical understanding of present problems—thus also contributing to fuel the public debate on those same issues.

Over recent years, we have been presented with architectural speculations sprouting from the most respectable, if improbable, sources. In the 1960s and 1970s radical urban proposals from the likes of British architects Archigram, or the more critically minded Superstudio, in Italy, responded to alarming developments of the so-called consumer society. Now, as exemplified by recent projections around the skyscraper of the future by a most important global engineering and planning consultancy,

architectural scenarios are resurfacing in much less avant-garde sectors. These are generally technological prophecies that may be regarded as optimistic utopias, or, otherwise, as perverse confirmations of a dystopian *dérive* in which the ultimate "sustainable" building becomes a fortified enclave for a wealthy minority.[32] Most importantly, however, multinational companies such as Arup now claim these design visions to be a direct reaction to processes of an unstoppable urbanization "faced with climate change, resource scarcity, rising energy costs, and the possibility of future natural or man-made disasters."[33]

The proposals included in this curatorial project are not that distant from such design visions, except in the point of view they adopt vis-à-vis a fundamental social imbalance that tends to remain stubbornly concealed. By way of design scenario tools, *Uneven Growth* participants were also invited to extrapolate from contemporary practices, current technological advances, and their own design and research experience. Their design efforts, however, were to be directed at devising situations in which tactical thinking was seen to provide social justice in the conception and appropriation of urban space.

The design scenarios presented in *Uneven Growth* counteract the dystopian outcomes that can be expected of the progression of current urban trends, both in terms of spatial segregation and of socioeconomic inequality. Even if they offer only acupunctural outlooks on how change for the better could be induced in diverse urban contexts, they aspire to solutions that could be replicated in different contexts. Moreover, they carry the belief that architects may indeed address urban inequalities and espouse a more conscious, if provisional, posture toward the future of cities.

As science fiction writer William Gibson put it, the speed of current transformations makes it increasingly difficult to retain a "place to stand from which to imagine a very elaborate future."[34] We no longer benefit from the "luxury of stability," which we enjoyed not so long ago. The future no longer being "what it used to be," the proposals in this catalogue and exhibition do at least offer partial glimpses of a desirable alternative universe: an urban prospect in which architects, artists, and other urban practitioners again meld social ethics into their much-needed aesthetic endeavors.

Assemble. Folly for a Flyover, London. 2013

Mahatma Gandhi Road in Dharavi, Mumbai. 2009

1   See Saskia Sassen, *Cities in a World Economy*, 4th ed. (Los Angeles/London/New Delhi/Singapore/Washington, D.C.: Sage Publications, 2012). This and following quotes pp. 241–66.

2   As Davis underlines, cities "have absorbed the majority of the rural labor-power made redundant by post-1979 market reforms," sometimes because the urban agglomeration itself grew to absorb previous rural areas. See Mike Davis, *Planet of Slums* (London and New York: Verso, 2006), 8–15.

3   See, for example, Akin L. Mabogunje, "Global Urban Poverty Research Agenda: The African Case" (paper presented at the Woodrow Wilson International Center for Scholars, Washington, D.C.). In this paper presented at the symposium *Global Urban Poverty: Setting the Research Agenda*, Nigerian geographer Akin L. Mabogunje analyzes the problems of urban poverty in the context of sub-Saharan Africa, the region that "presently has the fastest rate of urbanization in the world."

4   As we will see in the case of New York, social disparities and informal spatialities can remain invisible under the guise of the formal city. On the other hand, as a researcher has recently put it, "the nudity of poorly built environments allows us to see, clearer than in other urban environments, the mutations in the nature of social operation." See Eduardo Ascensão, "Following Engineers and Architects through Slums: The Technoscience of Slum Intervention in the Portuguese-Speaking

Landscape," *Análise Social* (Instituto de Ciências Sociais da Universidade de Lisboa, Lisbon) 48, no. 206 (2013): 153–80.

5   As Mabogunje reports, some of the most successful attempts to deal with urban poverty have depended on the mobilization of local populations through participatory strategies, as happened in the case of the Advanced Locality Management Scheme, in Mumbai, India. As the author notes, "such mobilization, especially when promoted by non-governmental organizations on a sustained basis, is expected to mitigate the social exclusion and marginalization of the poor and reduce their sense of voicelessness and powerlessness." See Mabogunje, "Global Urban Poverty Research Agenda."

6   See Robert Neuwirth, *Shadow Cities: A Billion Squatters, A New Urban World* (New York and London: Routledge, 2006). This is only one example of many recent publications on informal settlements in the context of developing world cities.

7   An interesting example of the current fascination with urban development is the attribution of the $100,000 Latrobe Prize by the American Institute of Architects (AIA) to "The City of 7 Billion," a research proposal by Bimal Mendis, Joyce Hsiang, and Plan B Architecture & Urbanism. The authors will study the "impact of population growth and resource consumption on the built and natural environment at the scale of the entire world as a single urban entity."

8   See Michel de Certeau, *The Practice of Everyday Life* (Berkeley: University of California Press, 1984), 18.

9   See, for example, Vishaan Chakrabarti, *A Country of Cities: A Manifesto for an Urban America* (New York: Metropolis Books, 2013).

10   With the African context offering the most extreme of examples, Mabogunje refers to the disempowerment and economical lack of local and metropolitan authorities themselves as one of the reasons for the inability "to respond effectively and innovatively to the challenges posed by urban poverty and poor urban environment of slums and shanty settlement." See Mabogunje, "Global Urban Poverty Research Agenda."

11   The literature being already vast, see, for example, the catalogues of three recent exhibitions on these subjects: Giovanna Borasi and Mirko Zardini, eds., *Actions: What You Can Do with the City (Comment s'Approprier la Ville)* (Montreal: Canadian Centre for Architecture; Amsterdam: SUN, 2008); Elke Krasny, ed., *Hands-on-Urbanism 1850–2012* (Vienna: Architekturzemtrum Wien/Verlag Turia + Kant, 2012); Cathy Lang Ho, Ned Cramer, and David van der Leer, eds., *Spontaneous Interventions: Design Actions for the Common Good* (New York: Architect Magazine, 2012).

12   Although this concept has been introduced by American urbanists Wayne Attoe and Donn Logan as a blueprint for interventions that take sizeable architectural structures as the catalysts for an urban renaissance—as can later be typically exemplified by the "effect" of the Guggenheim Museum in Bilbao—the notion of "urban catalyst" has been recently reassessed by other authors as referring to temporary interventions that reactivate urban voids and wastelands. See Wayne Attoe and Donn Logan, *American Urban Architecture: Catalysts in the Design of Cities* (Berkeley: University of California Press, 1989); and Philipp Oswalt, Klaus Overmeyer, and Philipp Misselwitz, eds., *Urban Catalyst: The Power of Temporary Use* (Berlin: DOM Publishers, 2013).

13   For a better understanding of the author's opposition of "strategy" and "tactics," see de Certeau, *The Practice of Everyday Life*, xix.

14   See de Certeau, *The Practice of Everyday Life*, xii.

15   Recently, British curator and writer Justin McGuirk has precisely explored the historical background of this proposition in the context of Latin American megacities. See Justin McGuirk, *Radical Cities: Across Latin America in Search of a New Architecture* (London: Verso, 2014).

16   This idea echoes British sociologist Raymond Williams's claims that high culture should embrace low culture in order to survive. We seem to be at a moment in which this type of conflation is again relevant. See Raymand Williams, *Keywords: A Vocabulary of Culture and Society* (London: Croom Helm, 1976).

17   As Michael van Iersel has voiced it, "technological innovation is rapidly changing architecture and urban planning." Yet, "in spite of the promise of more cost-efficiency, increased sustainability and improved esthetic quality, these new technologies can just as easily lead to the same kind of dull and dehumanizing spaces that emerged from the previous technological revolution called Modernism." See Michael van Iersel, "The City in Your Hands," *Domus* (August 2013).

18   The author critiques the current models of "intelligent cities" as missing the "opportunity to urbanize the technologies they mobilize." On the other hand, she proposes that "technologists, urbanists and artists are beginning to 'urbanize' technology" and this should be directed to "strengthen horizontal practices and initiatives." See Saskia Sassen, "Open-Source Urbanism," *Domus* (June 2011).

19   Urban strategist Scott Burnham proposes that, like computer games, cities "have their own unlock codes." As such, "resourceful planners and designers have begun discovering them" in the form of billboards repurposed as humidity collection systems, pavements wired for Wi-Fi, and other "increased capabilities." See Scott Burnham, "Design with Cities, Not For Them," in Architizer.com, accessed May 9 2014, <http://architizer.com/blog/design-with-cities-not-for-them/>.

20   This is the title of one of many recent publications portraying diverse incarnations of what is called here "tactical urbanism." See Marcos Rosa and Ute Weiland, eds., *Handmade Urbanism: Mumbai, São Paulo, Istanbul, Mexico City, Cape Town: From Community Initiatives to Participatory Models* (Berlin: Jovis Verlag, 2013).

21   See Julian Barnes, *Levels of Life* (New York: Knopf, 2013).

22   Rio de Janeiro was the stage of some of the earliest and most cited experiences in understanding the favela as an urban settlement with a potential for refurbishment while respecting the right of its inhabitants to remain in place. Consider, for example, the work of Jorge Mário Jaurégui, especially in his award-winning Favela-Bairro project. This Argentinean architect based in Brazil was also one of the participants in the exhibition *Small Scale, Big Change: New Architectures of Social Engagement*, organized at MoMA from October 3, 2010, to January 3, 2011.

246 Common Cafe. Food carts and farmers' market, Tokyo. 2013

23   As Saskia Sassen notes, "in a global age whose key axis is becoming the East-West rather than the North-South one that has dominated an older international colonial history," Istanbul's strategic location is "ascendant." Similarly, Hong Kong is presented as the "financial leader in China," due to "its open economy and its historical connection to international trade." See Sassen, *Cities in a World Economy*, 199–200, 203–4.

24   Shortly after Rio de Janeiro and Istanbul had been chosen as case studies for this project, violent mass protests erupted in both cities, triggered by government initiatives related to urban mobility and gentrification processes. In Istanbul, in particular, before protests assumed wider political implications, the population claimed their "right to the city" by contesting a plan to substitute a central urban park for a shopping mall.

25   Recently, an inflamed Internet debate on "slum-exoticism" and "favela-porn" was triggered by the fact that Hong Kong's infamous and now demolished Kowloon district remains a subject of research and utter curiosity about what was once the densest city neighborhood on the planet. See Guy Horton, "The Indicator: The Slum Exotic and the Persistence of Hong Kong's Walled City," ArchDaily.com, February 2014, accessed May 8, 2014, <http://www.archdaily.com/?p=481396>.

26   The two cities are between the four fastest growing megacities in the world, together with Dhaka, in Bangladesh, and Karachi in Pakistan. See "Urban Explosion: The Facts," *New Internationalist* (n.d.), accessed May 8, 2014, <http://newint.org/features/2006/01/01/facts/>. As the World Bank adds, the potential for growth in India's megacities is still explosive, as "less than ⅓ of India's people live in cities and towns." See n. d., "India's Urban Challenges," World Bank, accessed May 8, 2014, <http://web.worldbank.org/WBSITE/EXTERNAL/COUNTRIES/SOUTHASIAEXT/0,,contentMDK:21393869~pagePK:146736~piPK:146830~theSite PK:223547,00.html>.

27   Again according to the World Bank, although major urban centers in India generate "over ⅔ of the country's GDP and account for 90% of government revenues," slums still "account for ¼ of all urban housing." As for Lagos, it is the most crowded urban enclave in sub-Saharan Africa, a region in which, according to UN-Habitat, almost ¾ of the urban population live in slums. See UN-Habitat, *Slums of the World: The Face of Urban Poverty in the New Millenium* (Nairobi: UN-Habitat, 2003).

28   See Pedro Gadanho, "Emergency s. Emergency, or How Knowledge Must Follow Fashion," in *Tickle Your Catastrophe*, ed. Frederik Le Roy, Nele Wynants, Dominiek Hoens, and Robrecht Vanderbeeken (Ghent: Academia Press, 2011).

29   Bruce Sterling, "Atemporality for the Creative Artist," *Wired* (February 2010).

30   The introduction of the term "scenario" into planning and decision-making is attributed to American military strategist and systems theorist Herman Kahn, in connection with work done at the RAND Corporation think tank in the 1950s.

31   See Pedro Gadanho and Susana Oliveira, eds., *Once Upon a Place: Architecture & Fiction* (Lisbon: Caleidoscópio, 2013).

32   For such a reading, see the first of the micro-essays contained in my "Taken to Extremes," in *Beyond #01, Scenarios and Speculations*, ed. Pedron Gadanho (Amsterdam: Sun Publishers, 2009), 9–11.

33   See Nicky Rackard, "Arup Envisions the Skyscrapers of 2050," ArchDaily.com, February 2013, accessed May 9, 2014, <http://www.archdaily.com/?p=333450>.

34   See William Gibson, quoted in T. Nissley, "Across the Border to Spook Country: An Interview with William Gibson," Amazon.com, August 2007, accessed May 9, 2014, <http://www.amazon.com/gp/feature.html?docId=1000112701>.

THE CRISIS OF PLANETARY URBANIZATION

David Harvey

Concrete is everywhere being poured at an unprecedented rate over the surface of planet earth. We are in the midst of a huge crisis—ecological, social, and political—of planetary urbanization without, it seems, knowing or even marking it.

Protesters march toward the Mineirão stadium in Belo Horizonte during the FIFA Confederations Cup. 2013

On the night of June 20, 2013, more than a million people in some 388 Brazilian cities took to the streets in a massive protest movement. The largest of these protests, comprising more than 100,000 people, occurred in Rio de Janeiro and was met with significant police violence. For more than a year prior to this, sporadic protests had been occurring in various Brazilian cities. Led by a "Free Pass" movement that had long been agitating for free public transportation for students, the earlier protests were largely ignored. But by early June 2013, fare increases for public transportation sparked more widespread protests. Many other groups, including the black block anarchists, sprang to the defense of the "Free Pass" protestors and others who came under police attack. By June 13 the movement had morphed into a general protest against police

repression, the failure of public services to match social needs, and the deteriorating quality of urban life. The huge expenditures of public resources to host mega-events such as the World Cup and the Olympic Games—to the detriment of the public interest but to the great benefit, it was widely understood, of corrupt construction and urban development interests—added to the discontent.

The protests in Brazil came less than a month after thousands of people turned out on the streets of Turkey's major cities, as anger over the redevelopment of the precious green space of Gezi Park in Istanbul as a shopping center spread into a broader protest against

the increasingly autocratic style of the government and the violence of the police response. Long-simmering discontent over the pace and style of urban transformation, including the wholesale eviction of populations from high-value land in inner-city locations added fuel to the protests. Diminished quality of life in Istanbul and other cities for all but the most affluent classes was clearly an important issue.

The broad parallel between Turkey and Brazil led Bill Keller to write an op-ed piece in the *New York Times* entitled "The Revolt of the Rising Class."[1] The uprisings were "not born in desperation," he wrote. Both Brazil and

Architecture for a Change. Mamelodi POD, Pretoria, South Africa. 2013

Makeshift barricades in Kiev's Independence Square, during the demonstrations known as Euromaidan. 2013

Turkey had experienced remarkable economic growth in a period of global crisis. They were "the latest in a series of revolts arising from the middle class—the urban, educated haves who are in some ways the principal beneficiaries of the regimes they now reject" and who had something to lose by taking to the streets in protest. "By the time the movements reached critical mass, they were about something bigger and more inchoate, dignity, the perquisites of citizenship, the obligations of power." The revolts signified "a new alienation, a new yearning" that had to be addressed.

To be sure, the protests in Brazil and Turkey differed from the anti-austerity protests and strikes that dominated in the squares of Greece and Spain. They were different also from the eruptions of violence in London, Stockholm, and the Paris suburbs on the part of marginalized and immigrant populations. And all of these looked different from the "Occupy" movements in many Western cities and the pro-democracy uprisings that echoed from Tunis, Egypt, and Syria into Bosnia and Ukraine.

Yet there were also commonalities across the differences. They were, for example, urban centered, to some degree weakly cross-class, and even (initially at least) inter-ethnic (though that broke down as internal forces moved to divide and rule, and external powers exploited the discontents for geopolitical advantage, as in Syria and Ukraine).

Urban disaffection and alienation were quite prominent among the triggers as was the universal outrage at rising social inequalities, escalating costs of living, and gratuitously violent police repressions.

None of this should have been surprising. Urbanization has increasingly constituted a primary site of endless capital accumulation that visits its own forms of barbarism and violence on whole populations in the name of profit. Urbanization has become the center of overwhelming economic activity on a planetary scale never before seen in human history. The *Financial Times* reports, for example, that "investment in real estate is the most important driver in the Chinese economy," which in turn has been the main driver of the global economy throughout the worldwide crisis that began in 2007. "The building, sale and outfitting of apartments accounted for 23 percent of Chinese gross domestic product in 2013." If we add in the expenditures on massive physical infrastructures (road, rail, public works of all kinds) then close to one half of the Chinese economy is taken up with urbanization. China has consumed more than half of the global steel and cement over the last decade. "In just two years, from 2011 to 2012, China produced more cement than the United States did in the entire twentieth century."[2]

While extreme, these trends are not confined to China. Concrete is everywhere being poured at an unprecedented rate over the surface of planet earth. We are, in short, in the midst of a huge crisis—ecological, social, and political—of planetary urbanization without, it seems, knowing or even marking it.

None of this new development could have occurred without massive population displacements and dispossessions, wave after wave of creative destruction that has taken not only a physical toll but destroyed social solidarities, exaggerated social inequalities, swept aside any pretenses of democratic urban governance, and has increasingly looked to militarized police surveillance and terror as its primary mode of social regulation. The unrest attaching to dispossession in China is unknowable but clearly widespread. Sociologist Cihan Tugal has written, "Real estate bubbles, soaring housing prices, and the overall privatization-alienation of common urban goods constitute the common ground of protests in as diverse places as the United States, Egypt, Spain, Turkey, Brazil, Israel, and Greece."[3] The rising cost of living, particularly for food, transportation, and housing,

has made daily life increasingly difficult for urban populations. Food riots in North African cities were frequent and widespread even before the uprisings in Tunisia and Tahrir Square.

This urbanization boom has had very little to do with meeting the needs of people. It has been all about absorbing surplus capital, sustaining profit levels, and maximizing the return on exchange values no matter what the use value demands might be. The consequences have often been irrational in the extreme. While there is a chronic shortage of affordable housing in almost every major city, their skylines are littered with empty condominiums for the ultra-rich whose main interest is in speculating in property values rather than constructing a settled life. In New York City, where half of the population has to live on less than $30,000 per year (as contrasted with the top 1 percent, who had an average annual income of $3.57 million per year according to tax records for 2012), there is an affordable housing crisis because nowhere is it possible to find a two-bedroom apartment for the $1,500 per month that a family of four should be spending on housing given an income of $30,000. In almost all the major cities in the U.S. the average expenditure on housing is way over the thirty percent of disposable income that is considered reasonable.[4] The same applies to London, where there are whole streets of unoccupied mansions being held for purely speculative purposes. Meanwhile, the British

AFFECT-T. Bamboo micro-housing, Hong Kong. 2013

government attempts to increase the supply of affordable housing by putting a bedroom tax on social housing for the most vulnerable sector of the population, resulting in, for example, the eviction of a widow living alone in a two-bedroom council house. The empty bedroom tax has plainly been put on the wrong class, but governments these days appear to be singularly dedicated to feathering the nests of the wealthy at the expense of the poor and the disadvantaged. The same irrationality of empty dwellings in the midst of shortages of affordable housing can be found in Brazil, Turkey, Dubai, and Chile as well as all the global cities of high finance such as London and New York. Meanwhile, budget austerities and reluctance to tax the wealthy given the overwhelming power of a now triumphant oligarchy means declining public services for the masses and further astonishing accumulation of wealth for the few.

It is in conditions of this sort that the propensity to political revolt begins to fester. Universal alienation from a burdensome daily life in the city is everywhere in evidence.[5] But so are the innumerable attempts on the part of individuals, social groups, and political movements to find ways to construct a decent life in a decent living environment. The theme that there must be an alternative takes many forms and produces many quasi-solutions in seemingly infinite guises.

It is in this context that concerned groups of thinkers and practitioners

Protesters resist redevelopment plans for Gezi Park in Istanbul. 2013

are exploring alternatives, sometimes at small scales but in other instances, in the wake of urban revolts, to encourage the search for better forms of urban living. The do-it-yourself ethos of many social groups cast adrift from the prevailing dynamic of capital accumulation creates possibilities for alliances of urban thinkers and technicians with nascent social movements searching for a good, or at least a better, life. In Andean nations the ideal of "*buen vivir*" is implanted in national constitutions even as it conflicts with neo-liberalizing practices on the ground.[6] With massive populations deemed surplus and disposable in a context of perpetual land grabbing by developers and financiers, aided all too often by a corrupted state apparatus, many situations arise in which political battles take shape well before some fuse is lit to turn the growing propensity for street revolts into an active reality.

There are popular possibilities and potentialities emerging out of the crisis of planetary urbanization and its multiple discontents. This is so even in the face of the seemingly overwhelming force of endless capital accumulation growing at an unsustainable compound rate and in spite of the power across social classes being wielded by an increasingly visible and intransigent global oligarchy.[7]

So what is it that might emerge from the popular revolts? There are confusing signs and signals but also some important clues. In Gezi Park, for example, it was not only the park that mattered. The "rising class" constructed instantaneous social solidarities, an economy of sharing and of collective social provision (food, health care, clothing), of caring for others (particularly the wounded and the frightened). The participants took evident delight in debating their common interests through democratic assemblies, launched into discussions that went on late into the night, and above all found a possible world of collective humor and cultural liberation that had previously seemed foreclosed. They opened alternative spaces, constructed a commons out of public spaces, and released the power of space to an alternative social and environmental purpose. They found each other as well as the park;[8] They identified a nascent social order in waiting.

This provides a clue as to what an alternative might look like. The spirit of many (though not all) of these protests and the spirit within the pro-democracy and Occupy movements is to go beyond "the new alienation" that Keller senses is so important to construct a less-alienating urban experience. Visceral resistance to the proposal to pour concrete over Gezi Park to build an imitation of an Ottoman barracks that would function as yet another shopping mall is in this sense emblematic of what the crisis of planetary urbanization is all about. Pouring more and more concrete in a mindless quest for endless growth is obviously no answer to current ills.

But the "rising class" is not all there is. In Turkey the mass of the Islamic working classes did not join in the revolt. They already possessed their own cultural (often anti-modernist) solidarities and hardened social relations (particularly regarding gender). They were not drawn into the emancipatory rhetoric of the protest movement because that movement did not address effectively its condition of massive material deprivation. They liked the combination of shopping malls and mosques that the ruling AKP party was building and did not care about the evident corruption surrounding the building boom as long as it was

Architecture and Vision.
WarkaWater Tower, Ethiopia. 2012

a source of jobs. The protest movement of Gezi was, as the subsequent municipal elections showed, not cross-class enough to last.

There is no one answer to our predicaments. The urban experience under capitalism is turning barbaric as well as repressive. If the roots of this alienating experience lie in endless capital accumulation, then those roots must ultimately be severed. Lives and well-being must be rerooted in other modes of producing and consuming, while new forms of sociality must be constructed. The neoliberal ethos of isolated individualism and personal rather than social responsibility has to be overcome. The material needs of the masses must be met and combined with cultural emancipation. Taking back the streets in acts of collective protest can be a beginning. But it is only a beginning and cannot be an end in itself.[9] Maximizing *buen vivir* for all in the city rather than the value of Gross Domestic Product for the benefit of the few is a great idea. It needs to be grounded in urban practices everywhere.

David Harvey is Distinguished Professor of Anthropology and Geography at The Graduate Center of the City University of New York

Csutoras & Liando. Kineforum Misbar Monas, temporary open-air theater in Jakarta. 2013

1 Bill Keller, "The Revolt of the Rising Class," *New York Times*, June 30, 2013, A23.

2 Jamil Anderlini, "Property Sector Slowdown Adds to China Fears," *Financial Times*, May 13, 2014; Keith Bradsher, "China's Sizzling Real Estate Market Cools," *New York Times*, May 13, 2014, B1.

3 Cihan Tugal, "Resistance Everywhere: The Gezi Revolt in Global Perspective," *New Perspectives on Turkey* 49 (2013): 157–72.

4 Shaila Dewan, "In Many Cities Rent is Rising Out of Reach of Middle Class, *New York Times*, April 14, 2014, A1.

5 David Harvey, chapter 17 in *Seventeen Contradictions and the End of Capitalism* (New York: Oxford University Press, 2014).

6 Republic of Ecuador National Planning Council, *National Plan for Good Living: Building a Plurinational and Intercultural State* (Quito: Senplades, 2010).

7 The trends toward greater inequality have recently been spectacularly documented in Thomas Piketty, *Capital in the Twenty-First Century* (Cambridge, Mass.: Harvard University Press, 2014).

8 Arzu Ozturkmen, "The Park, the Penguin and the Gas: Experience and Performance in Progress of Gezi Events," *Mimeo* (Bogazici University, Istanbul).

9 David Harvey, *Rebel Cities: From the Right to the City to the Urban Revolution* (London: Verso, 2012).

ACCRETION AND RUPTURE IN THE GLOBAL CITY

Ricky Burdett

Both small-scale interventions and metropolitan order play their part in structuring social cohesion and engendering a sense of urban democracy. They provide opportunities for people in cities to make the most of their circumstances …

Pablo López Luz. *Vista aérea de la Ciudad de México, V.* 2006. From the series Terrazo, 2005–09. Digital inkjet print with Ultra Chrome K3 ink, 39⅜ × 39⅜" (100 × 100 cm). Collection the artist

The Museum of Modern Art's exhibition *Uneven Growth* and its associated design process recognize that cities today are being made and remade at a faster pace and at a larger scale than ever before. Yet the discussion about their future is lodged in an intellectual impasse that is, at best, fifty years out of date and rooted in very Western preoccupations about urban change (e.g., Robert Moses vs. Jane Jacobs).[1] Much of the discourse on the future of cities is trapped in a professional paradigm that focuses on the role of urban planners and policymakers, while everyday urban realities are being shaped by a very different set of informal processes and actors that are largely immune to planning and policymaking.

Despite the increasing complexity and specificity of the global urban condition, the old "bottom-up vs. top-down" model still frames the debate about how cities should be planned, managed, and governed. Through its multiple initiatives, *Uneven Growth* is a fresh attempt to reframe the theory and practice of design through the notion of "tactical urbanisms"

David Goldblatt. *Here, on 26 June 1955, under severe harassment by the police, some 3000 people from all over South Africa, met in a Congress of the People and adopted the Freedom Charter, which inspired the constitution of post-apartheid democratic South Africa. Freedom Square, Kliptown, Soweto, Johannesburg. 10 December 2003.* Digital print. Collection the artist

Le Corbusier and Pierre Jeanneret. Model of the Plan Voisin for Paris. 1925. Fondation Le Corbusier, Paris. FLC L2-14-46

grounded in different urban geographies and spatialities.

The intensity of *urban churn* currently being experienced in areas of rapid urbanization—from Mumbai to Lagos, Istanbul to Rio de Janeiro—or the need to *retrofit* more mature urban systems like New York or Hong Kong present a conundrum for urban professionals and scholars concerned with the interplay of spatial, social, and temporal dynamics. In fact, the planning and urban design professions seem to have lost the ability to conceptualize and implement robust spatial models that are capable of adaptation and change at a time when city dynamics are both volatile and uncertain, choosing instead to opt for anachronistic, unidimensional, and rigid urban models that fail to live up to the social and environmental exigencies of twenty-first-century urbanization.

The reflections offered in this essay do not belong to the conventions of empirical social science nor to the canons of planning discourse. They are based largely on the observation and analysis of projects, developments, and initiatives at a metropolitan level and "on the ground" in over twenty cities that have been the focus of research and direct involvement over the past decade.[2] The intellectual underpinning of this inquiry is an investigation of the links between social and physical dynamics of urban life, focusing on urban form and human activity.[3]

The experience gained from these studies suggests that the potential for social integration and democratic engagement of socially excluded urban residents is often realized through the type of small-scale "acupuncture" projects—implemented by a new generation of "tactical urbanists"—that succeed in bringing people and communities together in ways that formal planning processes

Danny Lyon. *Dropping a wall.* 1967. From the series The Destruction of Lower Manhattan.
Gelatin silver print, 12 ³⁄₁₆" × 8 ³⁄₁₆" (31 × 20.8 cm)

million people) lives in "slum-like conditions" while urban dwellers will continue to swell cities of the global South by 2050. In both Mexico City and Mumbai, for example, the same number of people who today live in New York City, London, Paris, and Berlin combined live and operate in informal and unplanned environments, without access to basic services or infrastructure. There is some disagreement among scholars as to whether such negative terms as "slums," "favelas," or "barrios" should be used to describe these informal settlements, which—to a lesser or greater degree—concentrate poverty but also act as repositories of human energy and ingenuity. In *Planet of Slums*, Mike Davis[5] is forthright in his accusation of what he considers an unacceptable human condition, while Doug Saunders,[6] in *Arrival City*, rejects the term "slum" and its connotations of abjection, hopelessness, and stagnation. In *Shadow Cities*, Robert Neuwirth[7] also rejects the term "slum" for its denigrating connotations, arguing that residents of Rocinha in Rio, Sanjay Gandhi Nagar in Mumbai, and the *gecekondus* of Istanbul have over the years improved their neighborhoods by investing in local environments, developing forms of "associational life" that make the most of human potential.

While these accounts do not define the role that space and design play in fostering greater integration and identity, they do bring into sharp focus the apparent paradox of codependency between the formal economy and informal development in many of these global cities, where homogeneous concentrations of "placeless" capital often sit cheek-by-jowl with the vibrancy of informal neighborhoods, providing cheap labor close to centers of power and production.[8] The social and political

have so uniquely failed to do. What is happening "on the ground" can be described as a process of urban integration that not only questions our role as urban designers and planners in terms of what we design and for whom, but also shifts the focus of analysis away from the rather blunt instruments of "top-down vs. bottom-up" planning toward a more nuanced understanding of processes of urban "accretion and rupture."

The overall statistics on urbanization are well-known. UN-Habitat[4] has calculated that a third of the global urban population (over 820

Serkan Taycan. *Shell #08, Istanbul, Turkey*. 2012. Archival digital prints, each 35⁷⁄₁₆ × 46¹⁄₁₆" (90 × 117 cm). Collection the artist

complexities raised by such volatile associations partly explain the inability of the planning professions to come up with credible solutions for how to deal with these informal repositories of human capability and their juxtaposition to the formal city. The "tabula rasa" approach enshrined in CIAM and Le Corbusier's Charter of Athens, where entire neighborhoods are demolished to make space for new, more "salutary" replacements, is the preferred model of "progressive" city leaders of the global South[9] just as much today as it was in the 1970s when Jane Jacobs fought her rear-guard action to protect New York from Robert Moses's demolition cranes. Ultimately, there is little appetite among urban politicians and professional consultants for the messy process of "urban retrofitting" of spaces and communities that have been espoused by a new breed of tactical urbanists—NGOs, activists, and increasingly engaged coalitions of academics, designers, and community agencies.

The identification of these complex phenomena requires a forensic examination that goes deep into the substrata of urban and social form, often at the more localized scale, where informal processes are at play. A few examples serve to illustrate this point. São Paulo, Brazil's economic engine, is expanding horizontally, pushing the most deprived outward

to its most peripheral areas, which lack access to basic services like sewers, clean water, and schools.[10] Nonetheless, concentrations of extreme wealth (often in highly guarded gated communities) coexist in close proximity to squatter settlements. Mumbai's cynical attempts to redevelop Dharavi, India's largest slum, located on valuable land near the city's center, with large commercial and housing blocks replacing the fine urban grain of one of the city's most sustainable communities, raises the specter of 1960s "slum clearance" programs that devastated the social life and urban structure of so many European and American cities. New residential or business districts on the fringes of Shanghai, Beijing, or Guangzhou, or new towns on the edges of Hong Kong, Cairo, Istanbul, Mumbai, or Lagos possess similar characteristics: large, monochrome arrays of "cookie-cutter" buildings—with the occasional iconic signature structure—surrounded by asphalt and picturesque landscaping, and designed to be "apart," new, and different.

This is what Ash Amin has aptly described as "telescopic urbanism,"[11] a form of intervention that relies on rapid

implementation of buildings and spaces that have little to do with the scale, texture, and fabric of existing neighborhoods and communities. Superblocks and groundscrapers that turn their backs on streets and alleyways, and housing, commercial, or leisure enclaves disconnected from their contexts are the hallmarks of this new urbanism: a process of "rupture" rather than "accretion." It is the more organic process of slow and gradual adaptation that characterizes many of the cities explored and captured by *Uneven Growth*, which absorb social and economic change without undergoing such radical shocks.

While scholars, planners, and architects continue to debate the connections between democracy and urban form, most would agree that time and appropriation are critical to the creation of a sense of collective identity.[12] We know how difficult it is to create an "instant city," with the overlaying complexities of urban life that Richard Sennett so accurately defines in his defense of the "open" city and critique of "brittle" urbanism[13] that is resistant to social and temporal change.

Many ideal towns built throughout the

TYIN tegnestue with local students and community. Klong Toey Community Lantern, Bangkok. 2011

Kohn Pedersen Fox Associates. Songdo International Business District, Incheon, South Korea. 2011

ages suffer from the same bland-
ness and one-dimensionality. Yet,
other less formal but nonetheless
"planned" ordering systems seem to
have stood the test of time, adapting
to economic and political cycles
in ways that have enriched the urban
grain, creating greater density and
complexity in the everyday urban
experience. A quick look at any
page of the A–Z map of London, for
example, speaks of the accumulated
narrative of time and space at the

local and metropolitan level. In
a similar fashion, the Nolli plan of
Rome, drawn in 1748, captures
the porosity and permeability of a
historically multilayered city, where
the interiors of public buildings
(churches, palazzi, monuments)
and the public spaces of the streets,
alleyways, and squares intersect to
create a seamless, open, and accessible system. This quintessential
"figure-ground" map[14] describes
the democratic spatial DNA of a city

whose form has accumulated over
time (under every type of regime but
democratic).

Over the last centuries, New
York and Barcelona have revealed a
degree of resilience: an urban form
that has adapted to the process
of gradual accretion and democratic
change without the need for "telescopic urbanism." In effect these
cities have been retrofitted over time.
While Robert Moses tried his best to
plow new roads and freeways for the

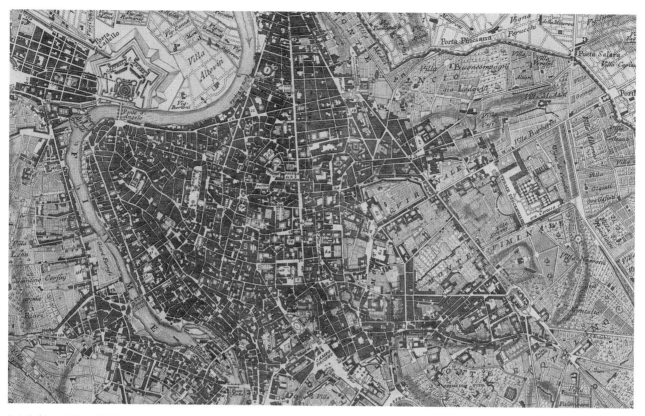

Detail of Ignazio Benedetti's "Nuova Pianta Topografica della Città di Roma" after Giovanni Battista Nolli's 1748 map. C. 1780. Print, 19⅛ × 27⅜" (48.5 × 69.5 cm). Published by Venanzio Monaldini, Rome. The Getty Research Institute, Los Angeles

city's urban districts, the Manhattan Grid remains largely intact, just as Barcelona has been able to continually reinvent itself without losing sight of its own metropolitan identity. In a less demonstrative way, London has gone about its business of metabolic adaptation following an organic, unplanned path for the last centuries, providing another model of urban resilience.

What these examples demonstrate is a malleable urban order that embraces change without causing fundamental disruption. A period of economic structuring, a change in political priorities, the effects of migration and global competiveness have all resulted in shifts and alterations, but the core urban structure has remained intact. As Suzanne Hall has noted, these urban structuring devices constitute a form of

"democracy in built dimensions, a common literacy which provides clarity without prescription, allowing enrolment through interpretation which absorbs epochal shifts and ultimately both recognise and absorb the small endeavour."[15] It is through this smaller-scale urban lens that cities are showing signs of vibrancy and resilience through different instances of tactical urbanism.

On the ground, other dynamics seem to be at work. The initiatives featured in *Uneven Growth* in the backstreets of Istanbul, Rio de Janeiro, Lagos, New York, Hong Kong, and Mumbai suggest a creative ingenuity that both fosters identity and promotes a form of inclusion among the most excluded. It is this emerging architecture of contingency rather than representation that has a greater impact on

the average Carioca, New Yorker, or Mumbaikar than any metropolitan urban policy or government plan will ever have.

Both small-scale interventions and metropolitan order play their part in structuring social cohesion and engendering a sense of urban democracy. They provide opportunities for people in cities to make the most of their circumstances, either by making small improvements that punch well above their weight in terms of quality of collective life or through flexible and resilient open networks that optimize the democratic potential of their urban residents. The evidence from these examples of tactical urbanism suggests that it has the potential to foster—rather than negate—capacity building and social cohesion. The evidence from large-scale metropolitan plans indicates that a malleable urban framework—broadly speaking an open grid—lends itself to a process of gradual adaptation which "absorbs epochal shifts … and the small endeavour." This multi-scalar perspective informs us that social processes are the outcomes of often hidden spatial narratives, alongside more conventional social science considerations. It also suggests that both informal actors and professional agencies play their part in making cities more just and equitable. It is perhaps the role of urban scholarship to bring these two dimensions closer together, both through a theoretical reframing of the contemporary urban crisis and by the identification and explanation of projects and initiatives that are, by default or design, changing our urban world. MoMA and *Uneven Growth* have brought us a step closer in realizing this intellectual endeavor.

Ricky Burdett is Professor of Urban Studies and director of LSE Cities and the Urban Age Programme at the London School of Economics and Political Science.

This text is an edited version of "Designing Urban Democracy: Mapping Scales of Urban Identity," originally published in Public Culture 25, 2 (2013).

1   Rem Koolhaas, "Whatever Happened to Urbanism?," in Rem Koolhaas and Bruce Mau, *S, M, X, XL* (New York: Monacelli Press, 1994); Tom Angotti, *The New Century of the Metropolis: Urban Enclaves and Orientalism* (New York: Routledge, 2012).

2   Much of the research has been carried out at LSE Cities, an international center based at the London School of Economics, and through the Urban Age program, both directed by the author (see www.lsecities.net). Findings of the research are summarized in Ricky Burdett and Deyan Sudjic, eds., *The Endless City* (London: Phaidon, 2008), and Ricky Burdett and Deyan Sudjic, eds., *Living in the Endless City* (London: Phaidon, 2011). In addition, the author has been proactively involved as an adviser on large-scale urban projects in London and other cities, including the 2012 Olympics in London.

3   The intellectual "project" draws inspiration from Richard Sennett's oeuvre as an urban sociologist and Saskia Sassen's concept of "cityness," coined to capture the fluid and indeterminate shape and experience of broadly non-Western models of urbanization. See in particular Richard Sennett, *The Conscience of the Eye: The Design and Social Life of Cities*, reprint (New York: Norton, 1992), and Saskia Sassen, "Cityness in the Urban Age," *Urban Age Bulletin* 2 (autumn 2005).

4   UN-Habitat, *State of the World's Cities 2010/ 2011: Bridging the Urban Divide* (Nairobi: United Nations Human Settlements Programme, 2008).

5   Mike Davis, *Planet of Slums: Urban Involution and the Informal Working Class* (London and New York: Verso, 2006).

6   Doug Saunders, *Arrival City* (New York: Pantheon Books, 2010).

7   Robert Neuwirth, *Shadow Cities: A Billion Squatters, A New Urban World* (New York and London: Routledge, 2005).

8   Saskia Sassen, *The Global City: New York, London, Tokyo* (Princeton, N.J.: Princeton University Press, 2001).

9   The new "Mumbai 2020 Urban Vision" developed by McKinsey and Company and commissioned by the municipal authorities of Maharashtra, for example, suggests that all slums will be replaced by affordable social housing by 2020.

10   Teresa P. R. Caldeira, *City of Walls: Crime, Segregation, and Citizenship in São Paulo* (Oakland: University of California Press, 2001).

11   Ash Amin, "Telescopic Urbanism and the Poor," paper presented at the IIS World Congress, Delhi, in 2012.

12   Paul Virilio, *Open Sky* (London: Verso, 2000); Judy Wajcman, "Life in the Fast Lane? Towards a Sociology of Technology and Time," *The British Journal of Sociology* 59, 1 (March 2008): 59–77; Suzanne Hall, *City, Street and Citizen: The Measure of the Ordinary* (London: Routledge, 2012); Rahul Mehrotra, "The Kinetic City," in *Architecture in India since 1900* (Mumbai: Pictor, 2011).

13   Richard Sennett, "The Open City" (Quant Foundation), see <http://www.richardsennett.com/site/SENN/UploadedResources/The%20Open%20City.pdf>.

14   Colin Rowe and Fred Koetter, *Collage City* (Cambridge, Mass.: MIT Press, 1984).

15   In conversation with Suzanne Hall, lecturer in sociology and research fellow, LSE Cities, London School of Economics, October 2012.

Al Borde Arquitectos. Vagón del Saber (Knowledge train), Ecuador. 2012

COMPLEX AND INCOMPLETE

Spaces for Tactical Urbanism

Saskia Sassen

Current conditions in global cities are creating not only new structurations of power but also operational and rhetorical openings for new types of actors and their projects. I see tactical urbanism finding...spaces that may have been submerged, invisible, or without voice.

Empty city. Melissa Moore. *Site Effect, (i)*. 2014. C-print, 35 × 35" (88.9 × 88.9cm). Collection the artist

Normative order built in stone. Hilary Koob-Sassen. *Syntax Octopus (X Axis side 2)*. 2014. Marble and steel, 120 × 240 × 36" (304.8 × 609.6 × 91.4 cm). Collection the artist

Cities are complex systems. But they are incomplete systems. In this mix lies the possibility of making—making the urban, the political, the civic, a history, and, I want to argue, the possibility of tactical urbanism. Complexity and incompleteness take on urbanized formats that vary enormously across time and place. Given such diversity, the tactical becomes a necessity—there is no definitive format. Finally, in this mix also lies the need to recognize cityness. Thus much of today's dense built-up terrain, such as a vast stretch of high-rise housing, or of office buildings, is not a city. It is simply dense built-up terrain. On the other hand, a working slum can have many of the features of a city, and, indeed, some are cities.

I want to center the concept of tactical urbanism, and the project it entails, in this understanding of the city because it is in such a space that this type of urbanism can thrive. Herein lies also the possibility for those who lack power to be able to make a history, a politics, even if they do not get empowered. Powerlessness can become complex in the city.

Urban Space Becomes Strategic

Against the background of a partial disassembling of nation-states, the large and complex city emerges as a strategic site for making new orders—spatial, economic, political, environmental, cultural. Under these conditions tactical urbanism should find a strong ground in cities for executing its project.

But there are major challenges that confront cities (and society in general). Key economic and spatial trends contribute to a disassembling of the old civic urban order. One challenge then is to understand the specific potential for making novel kinds of broad platforms for urban action, for joining forces with those who may be seen as too different from us, and for other such urban needs. Fighting climate change can bring together on one side of the battle citizens and immigrants from many different religions, cultures, and phenotypes. Similarly, fighting the abuses of power of the state in the name of countering terrorism can create coalitions that bring together residents who may have thought they could never collaborate with each other. And so could the effort to provide better urban conditions for the growing share of the population that is poor or becoming impoverished, as is the case with the modest middle classes.

What this emergent urban landscape points to is the fact that some challenges are greater than our differences. Therein lies a potential for reinventing the meaning of living in a city. The strategic importance of the city for shaping new orders rests in the fact that, as a space, the city can bring together multiple, very diverse struggles and engender a larger, more encompassing push for a new normative order.[1] Further, the last two decades have seen an increasingly *urban* articulation of global logics and struggles, and an escalating use of urban space to make political/economic claims by a very broad range of actors with very diverse claims, some just and some dubious. These claims come from citizens, from the rich and the poor, from national and foreign investors, from gentrifiers and social housing activists, and more. The materiality of urban space makes much of this visible, unlike what is often the case with national level outcomes.[2]

Where Powerlessness Becomes Complex

Current conditions in global cities are creating not only new structurations of power but also operational

Making presence. Evan Browning. *La Salada 1.* 2009. Digital photograph. Collection the artist

and rhetorical openings for new types of actors and their projects. I see tactical urbanism finding diverse operational spaces in such cities, spaces that may have been submerged, invisible, or without voice. A key element of the argument here is that the localization of strategic components of globalization in these cities means that the disadvantaged can engage at least one moment of the trajectory that is today's global economy and global power: it is in global cities that this mostly private and elusive form of global capital hits the ground and becomes concrete, and hence visible.

Today's localization of the most powerful global actors in these cities creates a set of objective conditions for engagement, whether those involved want it or not. Examples are the struggles against gentrification when it encroaches on minority and disadvantaged neighborhoods. I see here something I have elsewhere referred to as the capacity of the city to talk back.[3]

Such a city is also a space where the growing numbers and diversity

of the disadvantaged can take on a distinctive "presence" and in that sense, possibly, constitute a sort of political infrastructure for tactical urbanism. It is probably the case, or perhaps even inevitable, that tactical urbanism needs or contains within it such a political dimension—where "political" is meant to be a very broad term and not the narrow, formal meaning of a political system. This points to the importance of making a distinction between powerlessness and invisibility/impotence. The disadvantaged in global cities can gain "presence" in their engagement with power but also vis-à-vis each other. And while the literature on empowerment tends to reason that only empowerment counts, I think that gaining complexity in one's situation of powerlessness makes a difference, even if one does not become empowered. Only certain spaces enable this. For instance, individuals on today's quasi-militarized plantations are mostly going to be in a situation of flat powerlessness, where no making of a history or a politics can take place. Those same individuals in a city can gain complexity in their powerlessness.

The space can make a difference. Thus I have long argued that cities offer the powerless the possibility of *making* presence. Further, while many of today's urban struggles are highly localized, they actually represent a form of global engagement; their globality is constituted as a horizontal, multi-sited recurrence of similar struggles in hundreds of cities worldwide.[4] It points to the making of operational and rhetorical openings for new types of political actors, including the disadvantaged and those who were once invisible or without voice. I can see a tactical urbanism engaged in specific sites in specific cities also becoming a

global space along such lines of multi-sited recurrences.

These joint presences of power and complex powerlessness have made cities a contested terrain. The global city, even when it is not a megacity, concentrates diversity. Its spaces are inscribed with the dominant corporate culture but also with multiple other cultures and identities, notably through immigration. The slippage is evident: the dominant culture can encompass only part of the city. And while corporate power

Florian Rivière. *Don't Pay Play—Soccer.* Strasbourg. 2011

inscribes noncorporate cultures and identities with "otherness," thereby devaluing them, they are present everywhere. Power cannot escape them fully.

The Global Street: The Value of Indeterminacy in a City

Street struggles and demonstrations have long been part of our history. What is different today is that they are happening simultaneously in so many parts of the world and that

Making markets. Evan Browning. *La Salada 2*. 2009. Digital photograph. Collection the artist

Indeterminate space. Rut Blees Luxemburg. *Viewing the Open*. 1999. Photographic C-print mounted on aluminum, 59¹/₁₆ × 94½" (150 × 240 cm). Tate Modern, London

one basic component of the strategy is to occupy a critical space in a major city. This is why these very diverse instances make me think of a concept that takes it beyond the empirics of each case: the "global street."

I would argue that the street, the urban street, as public space is to be distinguished from the classic European notion of the more ritualized spaces for public activity, with the piazza and the boulevard the emblematic European instances. I think of the space of "the street," which of course includes squares and any available open space, as a rawer and less ritualized space. The street can, thus, be

Tapio Snellman. *Cubao Incision*. 2012. Mural for Epifanio de los Santos Avenue in Manila, Philippines

conceived as a space where new forms of the social and the political can be *made*, rather than a space for enacting ritualized routines. With some conceptual stretching, we might say that, politically, "street and square" are marked differently from "boulevard and piazza": The first signals activity, and the second, rituals.

Occupying is not the same as demonstrating.[5] Many of the protests of the past few years—Tahrir Square, Los Indignados, Occupy Wall Street, Gezi Park, Tel Aviv, and others— made legible the fact that occupying makes novel territory. Thereby it makes a bit of history through its active use of what was previously considered merely ground. Territory is itself a strategic vector in all these very diverse processes of occupation. In the sense in which I am using it, territory is a complex condition with embedded logics of power and of claim making, something that it takes work to create, and which cannot be reduced merely to the elementary facticity of ground or land.

I would think that tactical urbanism is partly a practice that involves occupying. To occupy is to remake, even if temporarily, a bit of territory, and therewith to remake its embedded and often deeply undemocratic logics of power. This begins to redefine the role of citizens, mostly weakened and fatigued after decades of growing inequality and injustice. Indeed, the occupations have revealed to what extent the reality of territory goes beyond what

Aplomb. Rut Blees Luxemburg. *Aplomb.* 2013. Photographic C-print, framed, 61 × 47¼" (155 × 120cm). Private collection, Paris

has been its dominant meaning throughout the twentieth century, when the term was flattened to denote national sovereign territory. Tactical urbanism can then be conceived of as a mode of making that is at once local and multi-sited in that it can recur in city after city. It can arise out of enormously diverse histories and polities.

An essential precondition for such making is the emergence of the city, in all its varied forms. Thus the global street is emphatically an urban street, not a suburban or rural road. Indeed, the larger space enabling this multi-sited making is the network of global cities worldwide, whose numbers are growing (now reaching over a hundred) in part as a result of the expanded territorial needs of global capital and global finance. Herein lies an interesting dialectic between the growth of global cities and the growth of multi-sited Occupy movements.

In this sense, then, the city also makes visible the limits *and* unrealized potential of communication technologies such as familiar types of social media. I bring this up because it seems to me that the frequent confusion between the logics of a technology as designed by the engineer and the logics of the users could be a delicate factor in tactical urbanism. The two are not one and the same. The technical properties of electronic *interactive* domains deliver their utility through complex ecologies that include a) non-technological variables (the social, the subjective, the political, material topographies), and b) the particular cultures of use of different actors.

When we look at electronic interactive domains as part of these larger ecologies, rather than as a purely technical condition, we make conceptual and empirical room for the broad range of social logics

Making space. "We were making it into a coffee shop for the neighborhood . . . and it was demolished," Xanthe Hamilton, May 2014. Melissa Moore. *Corner, (Granby)*. 2014. C-print, 35 × 35" (88.9 × 88.9 cm). Collection the artist

driving users and the diverse cultures of use through which these technologies get deployed. Each of these logics and cultures of use activates an ecology of meanings and associated actions; for instance, one project with great potential is what I think of as "open-sourcing" the neighborhood.[6] Seen this way, social media can become an effective third force in tactical urbanism.

Analytic Borderlands: Extracting a Space Where There Is Meant to be None

I want to conclude with the challenge of "making presence" in particular types of spaces. This is perhaps

almost inevitably one component of tactical urbanism both in its urbanistic and architectural instances. In my own work I have developed notions of rescuing presence from the silence of absence. One aspect of this work was understanding how groups and activities and events that are at risk of invisibility due to societal prejudices and fears become present to others like themselves, and to others unlike themselves.

What I seek to capture is a very specific feature. It is the possibility of *making* presence where there is silence and absence. For me, as a political economist, addressing these issues has meant working in several systems of representation and constructing spaces of intersection.

Making space. Hilary Koob-Sassen. *Paracultural Narratio (X Axis side 1)*. 2014. Marble, steel, and aluminum, 120 × 240 × 36" (304.8 × 609.6 × 91.4 cm). Collection the artist

There are analytic moments when two systems of representation intersect. Such analytic moments are easily experienced as spaces of silence, of absence. One challenge is to see what happens in those spaces, what operations (analytic, of power, of meaning) take place there. I con-stitute them as *analytic* borderlands, whereby discontinuities are given a terrain rather than being reduced to a dividing line. Somehow I am inclined to see tactical urbanism as finding its operational site, or one of its sites, in such intersections, which now func-tion as invisible or silent spaces, or as dead spaces, or as *terrains vagues*. Much of my work on economic glo-balization and cities has focused on such discontinuities and has sought to reconstitute their articulation analytically as borderlands rather than as dividing lines. What happens if we begin to think of such spaces as bridging differences? They become a kind of frontier zone, in-between spaces that are underspecified, ambiguous, under-narrated. These are spaces where tactical urbanism can thrive and make visible that which was experienced as a non-presence.

Saskia Sassen is the Robert S. Lynd Professor of Sociology, Columbia University and co-chairs its Committee on Global Thought

1   The emergent landscape I am describing pro-motes a multiplication of diverse spatio-temporal framings and diverse normative mini-orders, where once the dominant logic was toward producing grand unitary national spatial, temporal, and normative framings. See Saskia Sassen, *Territory, Authority, Rights: From Medieval to Global Assemblages* (Princeton: Princeton University Press, 2008), chaps. 8 and 9.

2   Saskia Sassen, "Destroying Neighborhoods, Buying Pieces of City Land," *Urban Controversies*, February 3, 2014 <http://www.urbancontroversies.com/destroying-neighborhoods-buying-pieces-of-city-land-two-faces-of-the-same-deep-logic/>.

3   Saskia Sassen. "Does the City Have Speech?", *Public Culture* 25, no. 2 (Spring 2013): 209–21; <http://www.saskiasassen.com/PDFs/publications/does-the-city-have-speech.pdf>.

4   Sassen, *Territory, Authority, Rights*, chaps. 6 and 8.

5   I develop this argument in *Art Forum*; see Saskia Sassen. "Imminent Domain: Spaces of Occupation," *Art Forum*, January 2012, <http://artforum.com/inprint/id=29814>.

6   A city's backtalk is one element of open-source urbanism: myriad interventions and little changes from the ground up contribute to making a city andtogether are evidence of a city's constant evo-lution ("Open-Sourcing the Neighborhood," <http://www.forbes.com/sites/techonomy/2013/11/10/open-sourcing-the-neighborhood/>). In sharp contrast, "intelligent cities" seek to mobilize technologies to eliminate incompleteness, and often keep command functions in the corporations that sell the technologies; see Adam Greenfield, *Against the Smart City (The City Is Here for You to Use)* for one of the most thorough critical analyses. The intelligent-cities model typically misses the opportunity to urbanize technologies, instead making them invisible and putting them in command of, rather than in dialogue with, users.

RETHINKING UNEVEN GROWTH

It's About Inequality, Stupid

Teddy Cruz

The critical knowledge of the conditions themselves that produced the global crisis should be the material for architects in our time, making urban conflict the most important creative tool to reimagine the city today.

As I begin these reflections on the exhibition *Uneven Growth: Tactical Urbanisms for Expanding Megacities*, it is important to critically open up the two main issues embedded in the premise of this show: What produced this "uneven growth"? And what does tactical urbanism mean in this context; what can it offer to rethinking the expansion of megacities everywhere?

It is clear that the celebrated metropolitan explosion of the last years of economic boom also produced a dramatic project of marginalization, resulting in the unprecedented growth of slums surrounding major urban centers. This dramatic polarization between enclaves of wealth and sectors of poverty has accelerated the urban asymmetry at the center of today's crises. In this expansion of the so-called global cities is contained the DNA of an oil-hungry urbanization that has detonated a worldwide selfish sprawl, based on the privatization and erosion of public culture and natural resources, while exacerbating the socioeconomic and demographic conflicts of an uneven urbanization everywhere.

Though the term "crisis" has become ubiquitous, we do not know how to engage it. In the context of these unprecedented shifts, we remain institutionally paralyzed, silently witnessing the consolidation of the most blatant politics of exclusion, the shrinkage of social and public institutions and their role in the construction of the city. So, before economic and environmental, ours is primarily a cultural crisis—a crisis of institutions unable to rethink the stupid and unsustainable ways by which we have grown and the violence this growth has exerted on our environmental and socioeconomic resources. It is within this radical context that we must question the complicity of

Urban asymmetry

Dubai and Tahrir Square

architecture and urbanism in this irresponsible urban expansion.

Today, we cannot begin any conversation about the future of the megacity without critically understanding the conditions that have

produced the present crisis. Since the early 1980s, with the ascendance of neoliberal economic policies based on the deregulation and privatization of public resources, we have witnessed how an unchecked culture

Urbanization on steroids. Christoph Gielen. *Untitled XI Nevada*. 2010. Cibachrome print, 20½ × 25⁹⁄₁₆" (52 × 65 cm). Collection the artist

of individual and corporate greed has yielded unprecedented income inequality and social disparity. This new period of institutional unaccountability and illegality has been framed politically by the wrongful idea that democracy is the "right to be left alone," a private dream devoid of social responsibility. But the mythology of this version of free-market "trickle-down economics," assuring the public that if we forgive the wealthy their taxes all of us will benefit and one day become as rich, has been proven wrong by

the undeniable evidence that political economists Emmanuel Saez and Thomas Piketty have brought to light. They have revealed that during both the Great Depression of 1929 and today's economic downturn, we find both the *largest* socioeconomic inequality and the *lowest* marginal taxation of the wealthy. These are instances when the shift of resources from the many to the very few has exerted the greatest damage in our public institutions and our social economy. The polarization of wealth and poverty in the last decades has

been a direct result of the polarization of public and private resources, and this has had dramatic implications in the construction of the contemporary city and the uneven growth we are discussing in this exhibition.

These questions have framed my thinking during the years that I have been researching the Tijuana–San Diego border region. It is here where one can directly witness how the incremental hardening of the border wall and the apparatus of surveillance behind it has occurred in tandem

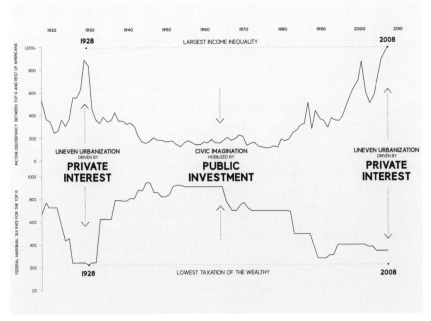

Diagram based on Saez and Piketty's study of American inequality showing periods where privatization dominates and periods where the public agenda defines growth

resolve the major problems of urbanization today, which are grounded in the inability of institutions of urban development to more meaningfully engage urban informality, socioeconomic inequity, environmental degradation, lack of affordable housing, inclusive public infrastructure, and civic participation.

The questions must be different if we want different answers, and contemporary architecture has ceased to ask critical questions (other than formalist ones) in the context of today's societal problems. This political apathy comes at a moment when one of the most relevant and critical questions in our time is: How are we to restore the ethical imperative between individuals, collectives, and institutions to coproduce the city as well as new models of cohabitation and coexistence to advance agendas of socio-economic inclusion?

So the rethinking of urban growth cannot begin without directly confronting socioeconomic inequality. And as a point of departure, this is a political project that contemporary architectural and artistic practices must engage, questioning the apolitical design agenda that neoliberal economic hegemony has imposed on the city, whose formal consequence is articulated solely by the protagonism of isolated architectural icons of beautification, supplanting many cities' commitment to an infrastructural way of thinking, whereby collective identities, the redistribution of resources, and modes of production can be managed. Finally, this shift from urbanizations benefitting the many into models of urban profit for the very few has

with the hardening of urban legislation toward the public, deepening the erosion of social institutions, barricading public space, and dividing communities. In other words, the protectionist strategies of the last decades, fueled by paranoia and greed, have defined a radically conservative social agenda of exclusion that threatens to dominate public legislation in the years to come. It is at this juncture, in the context of this sociocultural closure and the incremental privatization and erosion of public culture worldwide, where uneven growth gets specific.

It is necessary, then, that the political specificity shaping the institutional mechanisms that have endorsed this uneven urban development must be the catalyst for design today. In other words, the critical knowledge of the conditions themselves that produced the global crisis should be the material for architects in our time, making urban conflict the most important creative tool to reimagine the city today. Without

altering the exclusionary policies that have decimated a civic imagination in the first place, architecture will remain a decorative tool to camouflage the neoconservative politics and economics of urban development that have eroded the primacy of public infrastructure worldwide. It has been disheartening, for example, to witness how the world's architecture intelligentsia—supported by the glamorous economy of the last years—flocked en masse to the United Arab Emirates and China to help build the dream-castles that would catapult these enclaves of wealth as global epicenters of urban development.

But, other than a few architectural interventions by high-profile protagonists whose images have been disseminated widely, no major ideas were advanced here to

Adela Goldbard. Restoring an abandoned basketball court at the Old Officer's Club in Escambron, San Juan, Puerto Rico. 2013. Beatriz Santiago's Winter Session at Beta-Local

Tijuana–San Diego border

and cultural complexity embedded in the everyday. How to contact the many domains that have remained peripheral to design? Can architects intervene in the reorganization of political institutions, new forms of governance, economic systems, research and pedagogy, and new conceptions of cultural and economic production? It makes me think that we need to start by opening up and expanding our conventional modalities of practice, making architecture a political field and a cognitive system that can enable the "public" to access complexity, building collective capacity for political agency and action at local scales.

In this context, the most relevant new urban practices and projects forwarding socioeconomic inclusion will not emerge from sites of economic power but from sites of scarcity and zones of conflict, where citizens themselves, pressed by socioeconomic injustice, are pushed to imagine alternative arrangements. It is in the periphery where conditions of social emergency are transforming our ways of thinking about urban matters, and the matters of concern about the city.

So, while in the last years the "global city" became the privileged site of an urbanization of *consumption*, local informal neighborhoods in the margins of such centers of economic power remained sites of social and cultural *production*. These are peripheral communities where emergent economic configurations

also resulted in the erosion of public participation in urban political process, as many communities affected by this public withdrawal have not been meaningfully involved in the planning processes behind these urban transformations, nor have they benefited from the municipal profits they engendered.

What is needed is a more critical role for design to encroach into the fragmented and discriminatory policies and economics that have produced these collisions in the first place. At this moment, it is not buildings but the fundamental reorganization of socioeconomic relations that is the necessary ground for the expansion of democratization and urbanization.

It is within the specificity of conflict that contemporary artistic practice needs to reposition itself in order to expose the particularity of hidden institutional histories, revealing the missing information that can enable us to think politically and piece together a more accurate,

anticipatory urban research and design intervention.

But the formation of new platforms of engagement in our creative fields can only be made possible with a sense of urgency, pushing us to rethink our very procedures. From this emerges the idea that architects, besides being researchers and designers of form, can be designers of political process, as well as facilitators of critical collaborations across institutions and jurisdictions to assure accessibility and socioeconomic justice. I am arguing, in fact, for urgent experimental detours that might divert us momentarily from architecture as a self-referential autonomous field, moving from aesthetics for aesthetics' sake into an expanded, more problematic idea of aesthetics that also engages the relational socioeconomic

continue to arise through the tactical adaptation and retrofitting of existing discriminating zoning and exclusionary economic development,

Temporary installation by Jimmy Kuehnle at the Cleveland Urban Design Collaborative's Detroit–Superior Bridge MidWay Event, Cleveland. 2012

producing a new definition of the "political": that which emerges at the intersection between formal and informal urbanizations and the conflicts between top-down policy and bottom-up social contingency. It is from these informal settlements worldwide where "tactical urbanism" must take a critical position to elicit a new politics of urban growth for the contemporary city, taking into account bottom-up sociocultural productivity and stealthy, urban resilience as the agile devices to restructure top-down, unsustainable urban policies.

But as architects we are too often seduced by the "image" of the informal, seeing it as an aesthetic category only, without translating its operative dimension, its actual socio-economic and political procedures. The informal is not an image, it is a praxis: a compendium of practices, a set of functional urban operations that counter and transgress imposed political boundaries and top-down economic models. So as we return to these informal settlements for clues, their invisible urban practices need artistic interpretation and polit-ical representation, and this should be one of the spaces of intervention for tactical urbanism; or, put another way, how to engage the specificity of the political within the perfor-mativity of the informal as the main creative tool to expand notions of design? The hidden urban opera-tions of the most compelling cases of informal urbanization across the world need to be translated into a new political language with particular spatial consequences, from which to produce new interpretations of property and citizenship, housing and public infrastructure.

As we must strive to anticipate and generate more sustainable and inclusive forms of urban growth, the translation of informal urbanization's

tactical proce-dures can offer us a variety of critical provo-cations, culmi-nating here in a working mani-festo of equitable urbanization:

Architecture for Humanity. Mahiga High Rainwater Court, Nyeri, Kenya. 2009

— To challenge the autonomy of buildings, often conceived as self-referential systems, benefiting the one-dimensionality of the object and indifferent to socioeconomic temporalities embedded in the city. How to engage instead the complex temporalization of space found in informal urban-ization's management of time, people, spaces, and resources?

— To question exclusionary rec-ipes of zoning, understanding it not as the punitive tool that prevents socialization but instead as a generative tool that organizes and anticipates local social and economic activity at the scale of neighborhoods.

— To politicize density, no lon-ger measured as an abstract amount of objects per acre but as an amount of socioeconomic exchanges per acre.

— To retrofit the large with the small. The micro-socioeconomic

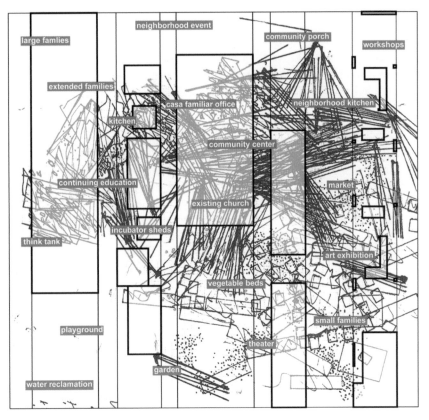

Zoning as a generative tool to reorganize socioeconomic relations at the scale of neighborhoods

contingencies of the informal will transform the homogeneous largeness of official urbanization into more sustainable, plural, and complex environments.

— To reimagine exclusionary logics that shape jurisdiction. Conventional government protocols give primacy to the abstraction of administrative boundaries over the social and environmental boundaries that informality negotiates as devices to construct community.

— To produce new forms of local governance, along with the social protection systems that can enable guarantees for marginalized communities to be in control of their own modes of production and share the profits of urbanization to prevent gentrification.

— To enable more inclusive and meaningful systems of political representation and civic engagement at the scale of neighborhoods, tactically recalibrating individual and collective interests.

— To rethink existing models of property by redefining affordability and the value of social participation, enhancing the role of communities in coproducing housing, and enabling a more inclusive idea of ownership.

— To elevate the incremental low-cost layering of urban development found in informal urbanization in order to generate new paradigms of public infrastructure, beyond the dominance of private development alone and its exorbitant budgets.

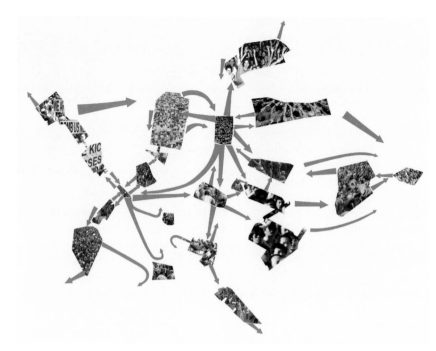

Debord(er): A neighborhood-based urban growth

— To mobilize social networks into new spatial and economic infrastructures that benefit local communities in the long term, beyond the short-term problem solving of private developers or institutions of charity.

— To sponsor mediating agencies that can curate the interface between top-down, government-led infrastructural support and the creative bottom-up intelligence and sweat equity of communities and activists.

— To close the gap between the abstraction of large-scale planning logics and the specificity of everyday practices.

— To expand meanings of spatial and social justice, understanding them not only through the redistribution of physical and economic resources but also as

being dependent on the redistribution of knowledge.

— To challenge the idea of public space as an ambiguous and neutral place of beautification. We must move the discussion from the neutrality of the institutional public to the specificity of urban rights.

— To layer public space with protocols, designing not only physical systems but also collaborative socioeconomic and cultural programming and management to assure accessibility and sustainability in the long term.

— To enable communities to manage their own resources and modes of production while creating multiple points of access to share the profits of urbanization.

These are the critical questions that *tactical urbanism*, in its most political version, can perform to

Community-based agencies can mediate the interface between top-down and bottom-up urban dynamics

generate "other" ways of constructing the city, through small, incremental acts of retrofitting existing urban fabrics and regulation, and by encroaching into the privatization of the public domain and the rigidity of institutional thinking. In fact, the role *tactical urbanism* can take is the mediation between top-down and bottom-up dynamics: in one direction, how specific, bottom-up urban alterations by creative acts of citizenship can have enough resolution and political agency to trickle upward to transform top-down institutional structures; and, in the other direction, how top-down resources can reach sites of marginalization, transforming normative ideas of infrastructure by absorbing the creative intelligence embedded in informal dynamics. This critical interface between top-down and bottom-up resources and knowledges is essential at a time when the extreme left and the extreme right, bottom-up activism and top-down pro-development smart growth, as well as neoliberal urban agendas, all join forces in their mistrust of government. A fundamental role *tactical urbanism* can take in shaping the agenda for the future of the city is to press for new forms of governance, seeking a new role for progressive policy, a more efficient, transparent, inclusive, and collaborative form of government. For these reasons, one of the most important sites of intervention in our time is the opaque, exclusionary, and dysfunctional bureaucracy, and the restoration of the linkages between government, social networks, and cultural institutions to reorient the surplus value of urbanization to not only benefit the private but primarily a public imagination.

Teddy Cruz is founding principal of Estudio Teddy Cruz and Professor of Public Culture and Urbanism in the Visual Arts Department at the University of California, San Diego

URBAN CHALLENGES
Specifications of Form and the Indeterminacy of Public Reception

Nader Tehrani

Architects are not just speaking to urbanistic issues in the traditional sense but to an urbanism of extraordinary dimensions and scope. Thus, the techniques and devices that form the foundations of this work cannot readily rely on received "urban design" conventions or toolboxes …

Mark Ericson. *Euclid's Wedge*. 2014. Digital print. Collection the artist

The theme of *Uneven Growth* is, no doubt, the result of certain urban and societal urgencies that are specific to our time—the radical speed of urbanization, the large imbalance between wealth and poverty, and an unprecedented scale of urbanization for which normative urban design techniques are less effective.

The theme should also be taken in a broader historical context to guide a new approach to the discipline of city making looking forward. First and foremost, we are faced with a situation where the traditional disciplinary boundaries between urbanism, planning, and geography may become a liability. The complexity of

the issues we now face requires the kind of analysis that is fundamentally interdisciplinary given the magnitude of data, knowledge, and emerging techniques that necessarily come into play when formulating a contemporary response. How the discipline of design factors into this process as a significant player is also in question.

Aerial view of São Paulo. 2007

The spatial, material, and formal aspects of planning cannot merely be indexed through the play of policy. Their instrumentality by means of design may be the precondition for rethinking urban and territorial strategies of the emerging city.

Central to the mission of *Uneven Growth* is, of course, the idea that the participants will offer not just analysis but also concrete proposals for various cities. This poses a twofold challenge: first, regarding the ideological nature and criteria of analysis as a launching point, and, second, the ability for design—through its instrumentality—to instigate change. Design agency is at the center of this question, as is how architects and artists bring to the table certain disciplinary traits and techniques that are not merely reducible to ideas, but ideas in the form of materials, spaces, and form itself. Otherwise stated, the argument is that forms, spaces, and materials are already culturally encoded with certain embedded ideas, and with the capacity to instigate readings as much as rituals—although not in deterministic ways. For this reason, it is necessary to achieve a connection between the architectural discipline and the instruments of social change, with a focus on how the techniques of the former gain a dominant voice in the shaping the politics of the latter.

The challenge, of course, is how to bridge the gap between larger societal questions, on the one hand, and the specifications of architecture and design that are often seen as arcane, hermetic, or elitist in their preoccupation with disciplinary peculiarities. Techniques and devices that define the instrumentality of design practices have quite a range, but they include practices such as formal composition, geometric patterning, typological transformations, material behavior and innovation, technological integration—or, more currently, parametric variations, environmental simulation—to name just a few. These tools are the prerequisite for architectural action and yet do not necessarily guarantee effective performance, cultural appreciation, or common reception.

The reception of the architectural discipline among a wider audience, for instance, is often fraught with an indifference to the very nuances of design practices, but nonetheless is central to its cultural relevance. The cultural warfare that is part of the reception by architects and urbanists does, in fact, require "the practice of everyday life" to gauge its performance, all of which happens in the context of broader economic, social, and political alignments. The theory of everyday life follows that none of the authors' intentions can actually be brought into alignment with the practices that occur in spaces. That is, in part, precisely the point: that the practices of everyday life bring a healthy and critical challenge to the dominance of specification, determination, and dictation. Indeed, one of the great contradictions of this research is to pit designers—as agents of specification—against a theoretical argument that challenges the very premise of top-down dictation—or at least gives credence to the idea that all that is specified will provoke misuse, appropriation, and transformation. As such, the practice of everyday life can be seen as the completion of the creative act, where the audience takes over the stage and becomes part of the mise-en-scène—unscripted, but even more potent than the screenplay.

However it may seem, my argument centers around the idea that our power as designers is, in part, due to disciplinary expertise, and it is its techniques that gain tactical relevance in the battle to project ideas about the emerging city. This, of course, does not suggest that as designers we do not have other forms of agency, but simply underscores how the peculiar tools of our practice have an embedded political capital. We must be aware that design operates irreducibly from a top-down perspective in its acts of specification, while its reception serves as a bottom-up antidote. The tools of design demonstrate, they prove, they

Anticoli Corrado, in the Sabine Mountains near Rome. From Bernard Rudofsky, *Architecture without Architects* (New York: The Museum of Modern Art, 1964), p. 36

construct alibis, and they qualify as much as quantify, but they do it through images, forms, and "constructs" that are not limited to words. It is these devices that help us to translate ideas to a broader audience.

In this context, it is also important to note that the convening architects are not just speaking to urbanistic issues in the traditional sense but to an urbanism of extraordinary

dimensions and scope. Thus, the techniques and devices that form the foundations of this work cannot readily rely on the received "urban design" conventions or toolboxes; one might need to develop an intellectual framework that is at once much larger than the city, perhaps at the scale of geography.

Of key concern is the challenge that once economics is gauged on the

Norry. 2010. Improvised bamboo train in Cambodia

global scale and once pollution and ecological damage is measured across borders—at the scale of the geographic—then one's design instruments would necessarily

Adrian Melis. *Vigilia/Night Watch.* 2005–06. Video: color, 5:30 minutes

need to accommodate an understanding of that phenomenon in commensurate terms so as not to trivialize the challenges of the megacity with the scale of tactical jewels. This is not so much a critique as a warning of the dangers of missing the larger picture or completely abandoning a vision of a larger order that may ensure the survival of scaled-down tactics.

It is, of course, alarming that with the rapid expansion of megacities there comes a deterioration of social conditions. The question is to what degree that is the result of design, urbanism, and the physical growth of the city, or alternatively to what degree it is caused by the lack of policies that are the preconditions for social welfare: access to education, health, and shelter, among other basic expectations. Bad design can be overcome with tactical alterations, but bad policies form a labyrinth of preconditions that defy the mobilization of the very social conditions we aim to challenge. For these reasons, while attempting to address a theme on tactical urbanism, one cannot fully disengage from a constructive dialogue with the contingencies that form the base of urban formations as well as the very policies that create the order of the city—even if centralized. If anything, the critical agency of tactical urbanism emerges from the adjacency it has with top-down orders.

If you like, the top-down serves as the host, and the bottom-up, its parasite. The danger of maintaining this opposition intact is, of course, to take for granted that there are no alternatives to the grand narrative that serves larger orders, on the one hand, and that the critique of power can only be done parasitically, and in some form of subservience.

In this sense, the very institutionalization of tactical urbanism at MoMA might mark the beginning of its domestication into a codified and ordered set of conventions, something the brief inadvertently or self-consciously professes—but it seems to do so also as something we can eventually transmit as a set of principles, with pedagogical ambitions and even a basis for policy someday, though it does not state this explicitly. Will the domestication of tactical thinking lessen its critical edge? Can it maintain its strategic position when it serves as a foundation for "best practice" in urban design?

Maybe so, but it suggests that we must examine what the status of "informality" is in this discussion. For instance, the informal tactics of urban mobilization, the result of Twitter and Facebook on the streets of Tehran in 2009, is one thing, and the aesthetic of informal decomposition as practiced by Sou Fujimoto is altogether another; I offer him as only one protagonist within this formal project. The former taps into the bottom-up guerrilla use of technologies of the day in the service of political action, which one can say in the process rediscovers the latent urbanism of Tehran. Tehran is revealed in the process but is not necessarily projected forward as having any formal ambitions; it does not enter the space of speculation but simply offers

High Line before reconstruction, New York. 2002

Sou Fujimoto Architects. Tokyo Apartment. 2009–10

a body on which social and political speculations find their imprint.

The work of Fujimoto, on the other hand, launches itself from the discipline of architecture, taking what Bernard Rudofsky called non-pedigreed architecture, an architecture without architects, to a state of self-consciousness, to the heights of artifice. Fujimoto takes what is historically developed as a consequence of organic urban growth as a starting point for a synchronic and artificial act: to compose informally, to develop new rules for informality, and to develop a syntax for that

Department of Urban Betterment (John Locke). Book Share, New York. 2012

which seems random. It is maybe poignant that Rudofsky's exhibition was hosted by MoMA in 1964.

Beyond the obvious and evident differences between informal process and informal product, as illustrated by the use of technology in Tehran and the use of composition by Fujimoto, what is remarkable today is the fact that the informal has already had a significant impact on our thinking, and has even driven projects such as the High Line in New York, a project conceived as conceptual, with a series of parasitical towers attached to it by Steven Holl, but then championed by a series of "friends," who in turn mobilized both bottom-up and top-down agencies to radically transform a near-obsolete piece of infrastructure into an active and critical piece of urban preservation, a testament to resilience. Here process and product come together in a more deliberate way, radicalizing the nature of both the artifact and the mechanisms that bring it to life.

The question of infrastructure should loom large in this discussion. Whether we are talking about the federal funds that are thrown at large infrastructural projects (top-down) or about the high-speed urbanizations already underway in China (again, centralized with a vengeance), both involve a level of growth, investment, and public impact that are

Tahrir Square in Cairo during Arab Spring. 2011

unprecedented in historical foot-prints. In both cases, the "public" is thrown under the bus, as it were—in the U.S. due to the the pattern of privatization that is the legacy of the last thirty years, and in China due to myopia, pragmatism, and ambitions for global prestige. Ironically, it is exactly in the area of infrastructure that tactical strategies become relevant for populations that do not receive plumbing, electricity, ser-vices, transportation, and for public space that is kept in the margins of architectural and urbanistic repre-sentation. Here representation is not merely symbolic but quite material, and a symptom of the very poverty that is the theme of this research. So, given the predicaments of this mis-sion, what do architects, as agents of specification, design? Do they design solutions or reveal problems?

Do they tap into the realm of infra-structure, opening up the design artifact for appropriation and personalization?

The other tactical route is to examine the legal edifice that builds the city as a juridical idea and to expose its forms; to do so is also to reveal its loopholes, codes, zoning constraints, and of course its exceptions and latent potentials. As it turns out, the bias of the law serves as an ideological ground that taints most urban policy and all infrastructural projects, and certainly gives form to the very city we are seeking to challenge. It is the white elephant in the room. For this reason, if the strategic developers of today use this very mechanism to build the city of privatization, why couldn't the same tactical thinking provide countermechanisms to

offer alternatives to the megacity to come?

The urban case studies in *Uneven Growth* provide for a rich ground of geographic locations from which to speculate. From Lagos to Mumbai and from Hong Kong to New York, all would tend to interpret culture, space, and the law in different ways. Of these cities, some will grow ten-fold with unprecedented speed, as we have seen in the past years. The challenges are how to mitigate this speed tactically, how to address the scale of the "mega" when one has no control of the centralized narrative, and how designers are to instigate change in the street without the strong arm of specifica-tion. If design's agency is precisely in its control of form, then how can one control its specifications while also developing protocols for its appropriation? How does one work within the law of design when being asked to work from the outside? And how does one avoid trivializing with a diminutive scale when the development of the city is forging ahead at a speed so raging that it poses the danger of simply running you over?

Tactical urbanism may be the material of guerilla warfare—the spontaneous combustion of a neighborhood built on unsecured property, or the takeover of public space, as we have seen in the Arab Spring. But techniques of warfare do not always work once a ceasefire has been secured. Thus, I would submit that a different form of tactical confrontation is also necessary once peace has been achieved—when common laws are put back into practice once again.

Nader Tehrani is founding principal of the NADAAA and Professor in the Department of Architecture at the MIT School of Architecture and Planning

Mazzanti & Arquitectos. Bosque de la Esperanza (Forest of Hope), Bogotá. 2012

DESIGN SCENARIOS

and Tactical Urbanisms

MAP Office, Hong Kong
Network Architecture Lab,
Columbia University,
New York

Swimming,
floating,
fleeing,
sinking,
how to absorb millions
of climatic refugees?

Hong Kong's natural setting is composed of 60 percent water. From a historical perspective, Hong Kong waters have continuously attracted fisherman, pirates, and shipping activities and continue to do so.

Compressed between sea and mountains, Hong Kong appears as a chaotic, hybrid, and colorful urban territory with extreme forms of density. Informed by a complex geography, the typical urban idea of concentric growth and continuous spread is replaced by a nonlinear development of hyper-dense cores coexisting with a natural landscape accounting for more than 75 percent of the total land mass. Framed by the city of Shenzhen to the north and the South China Sea on three sides, Hong Kong, 60 percent of which is composed of bodies of water, is surrounded 360 degrees by China. A collection of more than 250 islands, mostly inhabited, the city/territory is now under pressure from Beijing to absorb new waves of urban sprawl in order to accommodate a 50 percent population increase to the existing 7.2 million inhabitants. With the historical struggle for and stress on land resources, Hong Kong's geography is a narrative that is defined and redefined, again and again, according to political intentions and social and economical variations. Contrary to urbanism, it fluctuates in a conflicting appropriation of recognized land and sea.

Following MAP Office's recent project *The Invisible Islands* (2013), Hong Kong's composite territory may be understood through a new perspective: the possibility of populating the sea. The Anthropocene dynamic and the rising sea levels induced by climate change now provide the opportunity to redraw the geographical atlas of the world by altering the coastline and creating new lands. Man-made islands are a valuable alternative to support a sustainable urban expansion with new modes of living, working, and entertaining. Islands are paradigms of the living condition and as such can exacerbate the logic and characteristics of existing modes of production and consumption of urban spaces. Artificial islands are territorial fragments, yet they are constructed and destructed in a cycle that concentrates many of the forces characterizing human civilization. This cycle of production and destruction is a way to escape the present and to project the future.

With only 30 kilometers of land border in the northern part of the territory, Hong Kong is surrounded by water representing 85 percent of its territorial boundaries. Surrounding it on all sides, China situates the city/territory as an integrated part of the motherland.

Myths, legends, fictions, stories, histories—as many narratives as possible are required to define the contours of a new territory.

Until 2047, Hong Kong faces many questions related to its unique condition as a Chinese city outside the contour of the motherland. The possibility of an exponential population growth is a main concern regarding its future stability. Hong Kong's limited land restrains possible population growth to three options: reclaiming more land on the water, urbanizing the protected country parks—two options that Hong Kong citizens have long fought against—and creating artificial islands in

portions of the territorial water that are not yet exploited. In this context, Hong Kong could serve as a laboratory for an island scheme that could be extended to the Pearl River Delta and further along the coastline of China.

Hong Kong Is Land proposes to add eight new artificial islands to the existing landscape of 263 islands. In this way it addresses various needs and features of prevailing contexts as well as those of the near future. These artificial lands also provide distinctive hubs for tourism. Yet they cannot be recognized solely as islands nor generate maritime zones. More than a response to an unbalanced

geography, the eight corresponding scenarios can be interpreted as a new language in which to promote universal values. At the center of this project, beginning in Hong Kong territorial waters, there is a global awareness of specific contemporary issues that aims to reach other parts of the world.

The strategy of reclaiming land over water has been the main principle for development and for absorbing various waves of migration. This mode of operation, shown above, is now very much under popular criticism.

Since the early 1970s, territorial pressure has pushed the authorities to develop "new town" scenarios. At left, Tung Chung New Town, serving Hong Kong International Airport, emerges from the countryside park of Lantau Island. The new town appears as a concrete island to supply the growing demand for housing facilities.

The coexistence of rural activities with high-density living imposes a system in which the territory experiences extreme pressure. Countryside communities are in danger of disappearing. Above, the Lau Fau Chan oyster farm exists in the shadows of Tin Shui Wai New Town.

Density of building is one of the main characteristics of Hong Kong's urban context. The verticalization of living has led authorities to develop subsidized housing typologies that are now inhabited by 45 percent of Hong Kong's population.

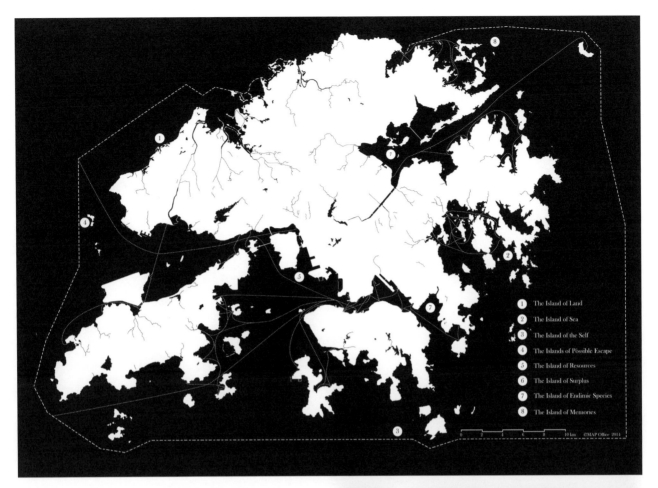

1 The Island of Land
2 The Island of Sea
3 The Island of the Self
4 The Islands of Possible Escape
5 The Island of Resources
6 The Island of Surplus
7 The Island of Endimic Species
8 The Island of Memories

0   2   4   6   8   10 km   ©MAP Office 2014

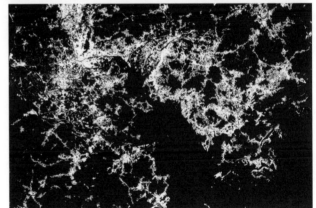

The Pearl River Delta Region, natural setting of Hong Kong city/territory, is among the most populated conurbations in the world. With one of the most important and productive global economies, the region remains dominated by its liquid geography.

The location of the eight proposed artificial islands across Hong Kong territory is based on a process of decontextualization and reterritorialization of existing life scenarios. Each island epitomizes one of Hong Kong's characteristic values from a territorial, social, economic, and futuristic perspective.

Water is an essential source of life and its access is a basic human right. "The Island of Sea" is a living organism merging an aqua-structure with a fishing community. Made of Asian vernacular architecture layered together, the organization of the floating village is directly inspired by the condition of its liquid environment. Here the water is the source of economic survival. This mode of aquaculture offers the possibility of a new economy and food production. Set directly under the house or to either side, seaweed and fish replace the fields the polluted land has lost.

"The Island of Resources" relies on the strong networking capability of the expatriate Filipino community. Through the collection and distribution of basic resources, the island is an asset to nearby emergency zones in case of natural or human disasters. Inspired by the form of a trading pit, it is an organic geometric structure suggesting a multi-faceted relationship between inside and outside, surface and volumes. At the center a crater—a dense place sheltering the most precious resources—defends its treasure like a giant safe.

MAP Office & Network Architecture Lab

"The Island of Surplus" in Junk Bay is an unstable archipelago made of a complex accumulation and compression of various types of discarded material. Fragments of trash collide in an entropically generated landscape. Abandoned detritus shaped by years of accretion resemble prehistoric vestiges of an ignorant civilization. Yet it is also one of the most visited parts of Victoria Harbor, with its unique silhouettes reminiscent of Ha Long Bay.

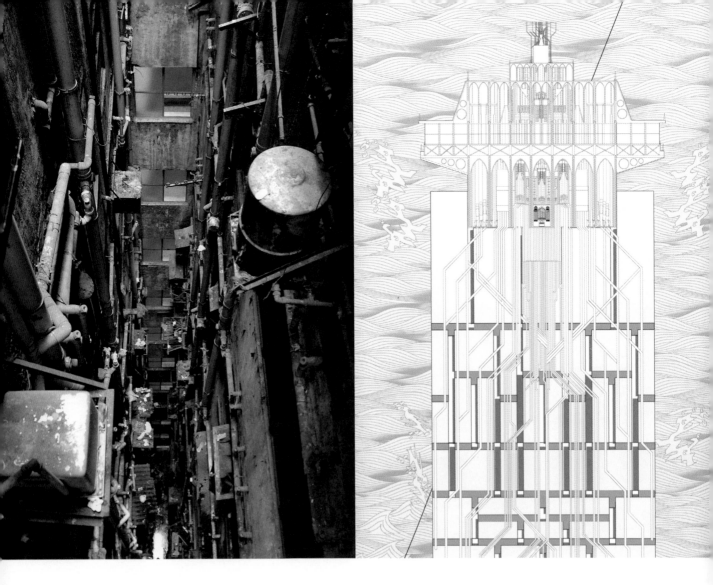

"The Island of the Self" is a floating
territory made of an intricate assem-
blage of alleys in the form of a maze.
Constructed as a supertanker, it floats
along the invisible borderline to the
south of Hong Kong, a no man's zone
where illegal consumption is autho-
rized. With tanks shaped in the form
of buildings, the island is made of
an infinite network of pipes, wires,
and gutters that serve as the main
organs feeding an intoxicated population. Dark and wet, the labyrinth
offers a secretive feast of drugs, adven-
ture, and sex.

75   MAP Office & Network Architecture Lab

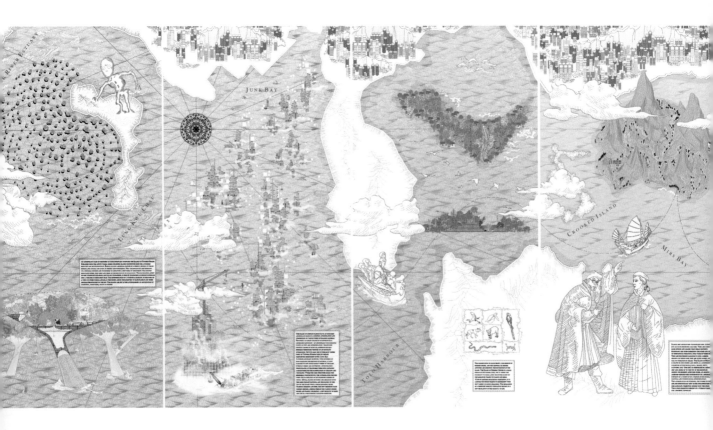

Hong Kong Is Land is a map of possible islands comprised within Hong Kong territory. Each island exacerbates a condition through which the city/ territory can be embraced from its past, present, and future; each island focuses on a specific economy, ecology, and community.

Uneven growth can only be solved through politics, but politics is broken when left in the hands of poll-driven politicians and screaming extremists. The *New City Reader* is a tactical newspaper installed in a public space that asks us to slow down, stop looking at our electronic devices, and once again read and discuss matters civilly in public. Based on the Chinese *dazibao*, handmade newspapers posted in public during the Cultural Revolution, the *New City Reader* is intended to be hung throughout the city—it is a tactical intervention that anyone can do.

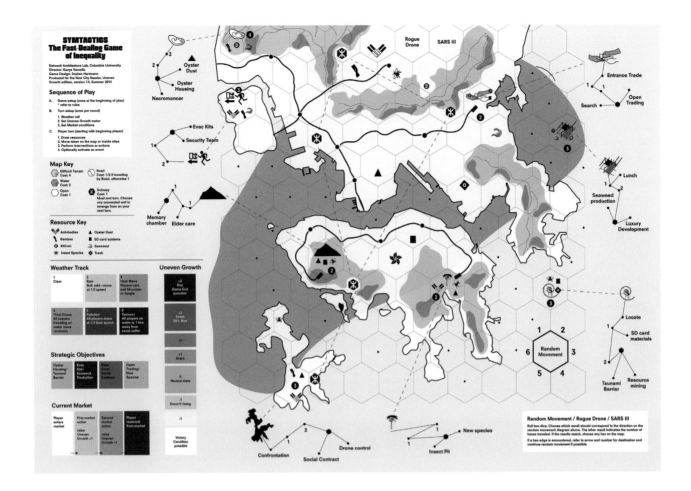

Included for free in the Hong Kong edition of the *New City Reader*, SYMTACTICS is a board game that teaches individuals to explore the relationship between strategic and tactical thinking as players race around a dystopian Hong Kong of the near future. As in other games, players are able to explore and work through the concerns of a given social setting.

Just as "The Landlord's Game," patented in 1904 and a precursor to Monopoly, taught people about the problems generated by accumulated wealth, SYMTACTICS allows anyone to try their hand at lowering inequality through the completion of tactical interventions while fending off challenges from outside forces.

TACTICAL URBANISMS: EAST ASIA

thecaveworkshop. Wave of Growth, Hong Kong. 2012

HK Honey. HK Farm, Ngau Tau Kok, Kowloon East, Hong Kong. 2012

Didier Faustino. *Double Happiness.* 2009. The Museum of Modern Art, New York. Architecture & Design Purchase Fund

Dai Haifei/standardarchitecture. Egg House, Beijing. 2010

ENCORE HEUREUX + G.studio. Room-Room for Paris, Beijing, Barcelona, Munich, and Strasbourg. 2008–14

Daiken-met Architects/Nawakenji-m. Sugoroku Office, Gifu, Japan. 2011

Eltono. 1/1 Project, Caochangdi, Beijing. 2012

John Lin and Olivier Ottevaere. The Pinch Library and Community Center, Yunnan Province, China. 2012

Shigeru Ban Architects. Hualin Temporary Elementary School, Chengdu, China. 2008

MAD Architects. Hutong Bubble 32, Beijing. 2009

Toshiko Horiuchi MacAdam and Interplay. *Wonder Space II* at the Hakone Open-Air Museum, Japan. 2009

West 8. Garden of 10,000 Bridges, Xi'an, China. 2011

WEAK! Architects (Hsieh Ying-Chun, Roan Ching-Yueh, and Marco Casagrande). Bug Dome, Shenzhen. 2009

William Lim of CL3. West Kowloon Bamboo Theater, Hong Kong. 2013

For more information:
http://unevengrowth.moma.org

ISTANBUL

Superpool, Istanbul
Atelier d'Architecture
Autogérée, Paris

Working with different scales
and levels of resilient action,
we imagine tactics for post-urban
development in which the
current TOKI mass housing
is animated by an open-source,
citizen-driven regeneration.

TOKI mass housing development, Istanbul

Turkey is currently one of the fastest-growing economies in Europe. Istanbul, with its 14 million inhabitants and a yearly growth rate of 3.5 percent, has fully benefited from this economic boom. Starting in the 1960s, its rapid urbanization has had three main phases:

Gecekondu: Early village-like developments on squatted land were the first response to the housing shortage in the growing industrial city.

Post-*gecekondu*: Starting in the 1970s, most of the *gecekondu* plots were legalized and granted additional building rights.

Mass housing: Since the 1990s, Istanbul has had unprecedented mass housing development. This process, which differs from earlier phases based on "self-building," is organized predominantly through the Housing Development Agency of Turkey, Toplu Konut İdaresi Başkanlığı (TOKI), in partnership with larger private enterprises. TOKI was established in 1984 in order to act as the public landowner and stakeholder in private developments or as the public developer of mass housing. TOKI has predominantly used a single urban typology: clusters of towers on open land, resulting in gated complexes with surrounding protective walls. The private sector has also adopted this typology to build repetitive fifteen-story towers, which are perceived as most efficient and profitable.

TOKI development parallels the emergence of a new middle class as a dominant class in Istanbul, which reflects a worldwide condition within global capitalism. Our proposal addresses the uneven growth of this middle class's aspiration to consume and live comfortably despite ecological and social costs.

Continuous advertisement campaigns on mass media construct a normative dream for Turkish families: car ownership and a condominium comfortably decorated and equipped with the latest domestic technology. A TOKI flat is the first step in realizing this dream even if the price to pay is isolation, reduced social relations, long journeys to work, hours spent in traffic jams or shopping in massive malls, high service and maintenance fees, and long-term debt.

As seen in Greece, Spain, Argentina, and many other countries affected by global crises, this deeply indebted middle class is the most vulnerable social group in a recession period. With deepening fuel depletion and resource scarcity, one can imagine that the positive economic curve in Turkey will likewise start to inflect, while forecasting similar impending

Invasive urban sprawl

Since 1975, urban developments have reduced green space and have begun to affect water reservoirs

Housing development mutations

Gecekondu (1960s to 1970s)　　Post-gecekondu (1970s to 1990s)　　Mass housing (1990s to present)

TOKI complexes on the outskirts of Istanbul

political, economic, or ecological problems due to global dynamics such as climate change. Under such circumstances, the current consumerist lifestyle will collapse, and the middle class of today might well become the poor of tomorrow. Faced with massive debt, growing unemployment, and increased costs for energy, fuel, food, and services, the TOKI inhabitants will have to become resilient.

Our proposal, Kolektif İşbirlikçi Toplum Oluşumu/The Collective and Collaborative Agency (KITO), is a post-urban development agency, which proposes an alternative positive scenario for the future of TOKI complexes. We imagine the current TOKI mass housing animated by an open-source, citizen-driven *R-Urban* regeneration. KITO will work at different scales and provide multiple levels of resilient action. It will conduct the coproduction of a number of retrofitted spaces, equipments, services, and institutions.

KITO's collective interaction and communication will be facilitated via an online network—KITO'da—which will create an alternative economy, assigning value to local actions and empowering people to make, give, share, and save energy, services, goods, knowledge, and skills. New individual and collective profiles will emerge to increase motivation and facilitate further civic actions: instead of consuming the city, residents will now resiliently coproduce it.

Consumption patterns of the emerging middle class in Istanbul

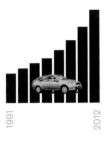

1991

2012

300 percent more cars in the
last two decades

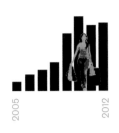

2005

2012

Seven times more debt in the
last seven years

8,1%

91,9% TV
WATCHERS

91 percent TV watchers

Global crisis

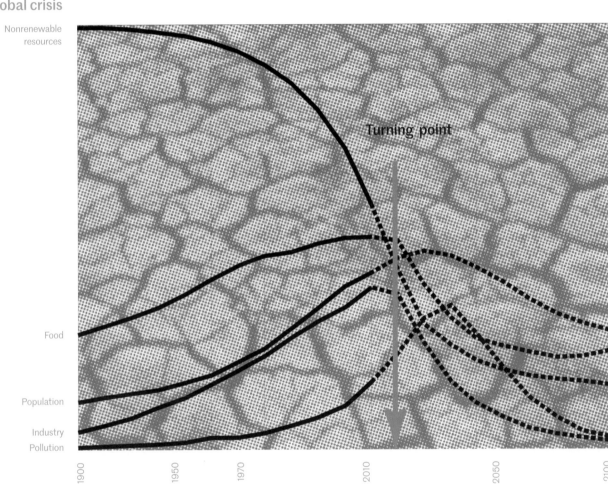

Nonrenewable
resources

Turning point

Food

Population

Industry
Pollution

1900   1950   1970   2010   2050   2100

Predicaments based on Limits to Growth—the
famous 1972 MIT report for Club of Rome,
whose projections on the end of global economic
growth around the second decade of the
twenty-first century were confirmed by recent
scientific reports.

Kolektif İşbirlikçi Toplum Oluşumu/
The Collective and Collaborative
Agency (KITO) will be set up for the
post-urban development of TOKI
estates. KITO is a citizen-driven, open-
source regeneration process, which
implies different scales and levels of
resilient action, and the coproduction
of a number of retrofitted spaces,
equipments, services, and institutions.

KITO region (right): *R-Urban farms* will
be created to accommodate green and
blue infrastructure (cultivation plots,
pastures and forests, ponds and fisher-
ies, rivers, canals) as well as
green energy infrastructure (solar and
wind farms). A number of communal
institutions and agencies such as community land trusts, credit unions, and
local development banks, will emerge
to allow citizens to act as collective
investors, managers, and stakeholders
for these facilities and services.

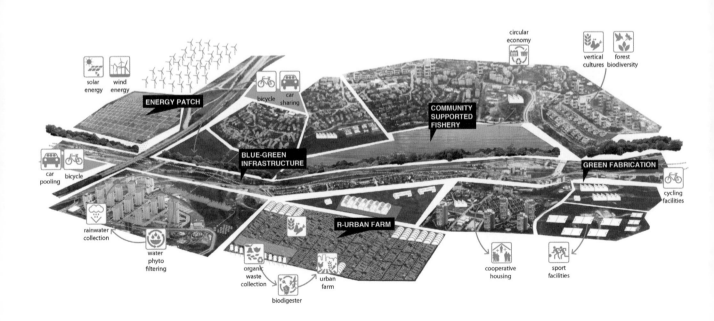

solar energy · wind energy · ENERGY PATCH · bicycle · car sharing · circular economy · vertical cultures · forest biodiversity

car pooling · bicycle · BLUE-GREEN INFRASTRUCTURE · COMMUNITY SUPPORTED FISHERY · GREEN FABRICATION · cycling facilities

rainwater collection · water phyto filtering · organic waste collection · biodigester · urban farm · R-URBAN FARM · cooperative housing · sport facilities

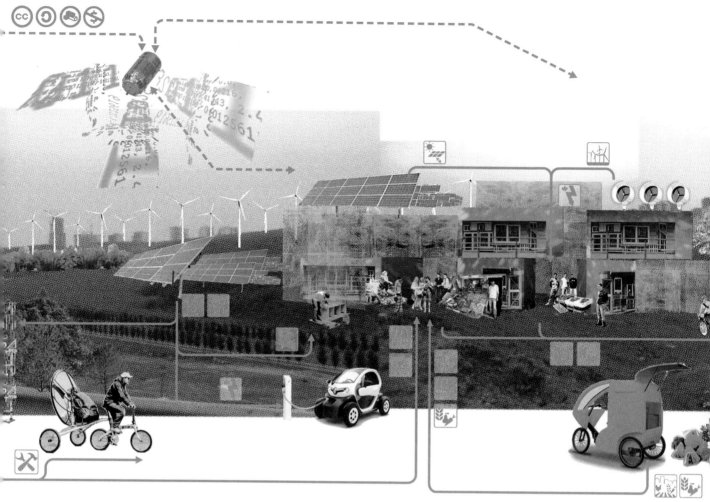

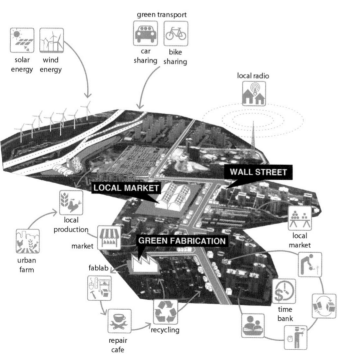

solar energy

wind energy

green transport

car sharing

bike sharing

local radio

WALL STREET

LOCAL MARKET

local production

market

GREEN FABRICATION

urban farm

fablab

local market

repair cafe

recycling

time bank

KITO neighborhood: The existing fences and enclosing walls of the TOKI complexes will be transformed into spaces for self-provided services: *wall streets*. The new facilities will be self-built by residents through 3-D printing and will host production, service, and distribution activities such as social enterprises, time banks, local shops and markets, fab labs, and local radio.

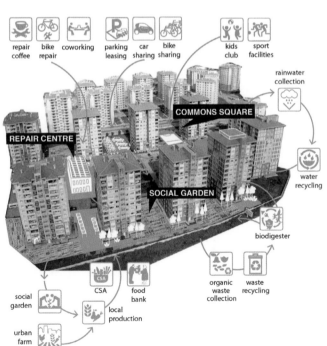

repair coffee | bike repair | coworking | parking leasing | car sharing | bike sharing | kids club | sport facilities

rainwater collection

COMMONS SQUARE

REPAIR CENTRE

water recycling

SOCIAL GARDEN

biodigester

organic waste collection | waste recycling

social garden

urban farm

CSA | food bank

local production

KITO compound: Neighbors will transform their central space in each TOKI complex into a *commons,* where gardening, repairing, and recycling will take place as well as energy production from collectively collected, organic waste.

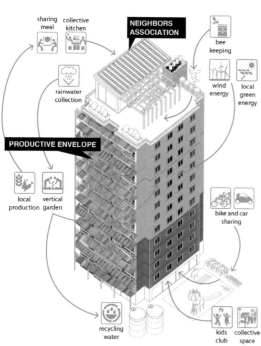

sharing meal / collective kitchen

NEIGHBORS ASSOCIATION

bee keeping

rainwater collection

wind energy / local green energy

PRODUCTIVE ENVELOPE

local production / vertical garden

bike and car sharing

recycling water

kids club / collective space

KITO building: Balconies, roofs, and terraces can be transformed into *productive envelopes*, which will produce food and energy and collect water. These will be managed by a neighborhood association.

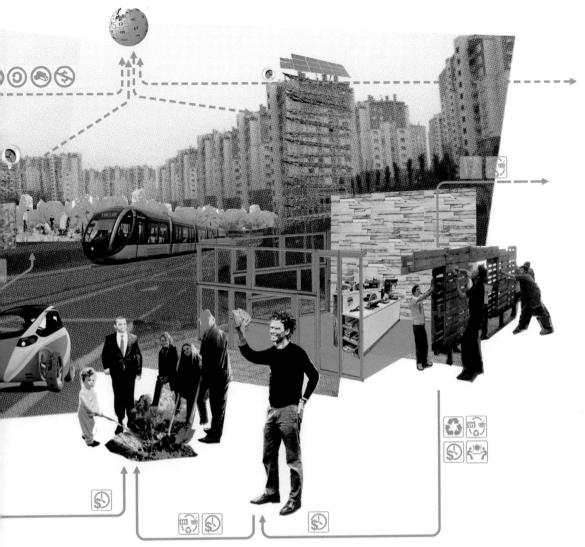

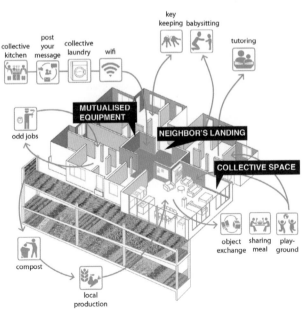

collective kitchen

post your message

collective laundry

wifi

key keeping babysitting

tutoring

MUTUALISED EQUIPMENT

odd jobs

NEIGHBOR'S LANDING

COLLECTIVE SPACE

object exchange

sharing meal

play-ground

compost

local production

KITO next-door: Stair landings and corridors connecting flats on the same level can become friendly common spaces—*neighbors' landings*—where activities and services can be shared, such as compost making, babysitting, and meal sharing.

KITO actions: Citizens will be prompted to act directly and online.

KITO'da: An online network that facilitates collective interaction and communication. KITO'da creates an alternative economy, assigning value to local actions and empowering people to make, give, share, and save energy, services, goods, knowledge, and skills. For example, this is how Emre started using KITO'da:

Emre is living in Kayabaşı, Unit A31/25. He has grown up in Istanbul's historic core and had to move to Kayabaşı because of his new job. He was skeptical; some of these neighborhoods had problems with juvenile crime. With some effort, he found a flat in an active community. He had not needed to be an active neighbor while living with his parents and was not sure how to become one. He signed up on KITO'da and used the tutorial to learn about opportunities for making, giving, sharing, and saving. Since the early 2020s, KITO had offered a shop in the compound wall to each flat in order to trigger social and economic exchange. Emre decided that in his wall shop he could store the books he inherited from his grandfather and let other neighbors use them as well.

This would be easy enough for him to do and would qualify as sharing activity. Nowadays, he uses the wall shop more often and opens it up every Wednesday for book exchanges. That's how he met Gizem, who keeps the unit next to his; she is good with plants, grows herbs, and sells her grandmother's garden produce periodically. Emre was also happy that his building successfully implemented a waste reduction campaign. The municipality awarded these efforts with free utilities for the following year. The money saved will go toward upgrading the compound playground.

For more information please see: https://vimeo.com/99619148.

TACTICAL URBANISMS: EUROPE

Karl Philips. *Good/Bad/Ugly*. 2012

Maria Papadimitriou. Hotel Grande—The Restaurant, Larisa, Greece. 2005

Beforelight. Under a different light @ Syn-oikia Pittaki. 2012–13. Imagine the City, Athens

Ragnhild Lübbert Terpling. Urban Rough Sleeper, Aarhus, Denmark. 2013

NL Architects/Gen Yamamoto. Moving Forest, Amsterdam. 2008

Gravalosdimonte Arquitectos (Patrizia Di Monte and Ignacio Grávalos). Estonoesunsolar, Zaragoza, Spain. 2009

VIVIAMOLAq. Parcobaleno, Santa Rufina, L'Aquila, Italy. 2012–13

Stéphane Malka Architecture. A-Kamp47
Stealth Shelters, Marseille, France. 2013

The Decorators with Atelier ChanChan.
Ridley's Restaurant, Dalston, London.
2011

Thomas Hirschhorn. *The Bijlmer Spinoza-
Festival* (2009) and *Spinoza-Car* (2009),
Amsterdam

Stiftung FREIZEIT. *Biographie einer
Stadt*. Hall in Tirol, Austria. 2014

Hotel? Wilhelmsburg, Neighborhood's
University, Hamburg. 2009–13

Recetas Urbanas–Santiago Cirugeda.
Nau de les Arts/ProyectaLab,
Benicàssim, Spain. 2010

Oliver Schau. DN-100 urban furniture,
Hamburg. 2011

For more information:
http://unevengrowth.moma.org

LAGOS

NLÉ, Lagos and Amsterdam
Zoohaus/Inteligencias Colectivas, Madrid

To bridge enormous physical and socioeconomic gaps, we examine three common challenges in Lagos—energy supply, water supply, and transportation—and rethink them as opportunities through new prototypes, urban infrastructures, and local collective intelligence.

Makoko and the 3rd Mainland Bridge, facing Lagos Island. 2009

Nigeria, Africa's largest economy and most populous country, is a region inhabited by over 170 million people. Its commercial capital, Lagos, is located in the smallest yet densest of its states, which is home to about 20 million people, of which a significant fraction lives in unplanned settlements with little formal infrastructure. Regardless, Lagos remains an equatorial melting pot and paradigmatic mix of traditions, a place where history, culture, and popular wisdom are interwoven with local knowledge and global awareness.

Although uneven growth is apparent in the nodal city of Lagos, challenges remain common for all Lagosians, regardless of their social or economic status. While oil is relatively cheap in Nigeria, the energy network provided by the state is only reliable for three hours per day. Independent of size or status, most homes, businesses, or facilities depend almost entirely on generators as the only reliable source of electricity. "What is the size of your generator?" is a common question.

Nearly 30 percent of Lagos state is covered by water. Water is an asset, yet highly underutilized. With the increasing impact of climate change, heavy rainstorms and ocean surges result in frequent flooding, which the city's poor water drainage system fails to cope with. The myth remains that Lagosians are afraid of water, when in reality they mostly live in water; as the Afrobeat legend Fela Kuti sang, "Water no get enemy" (Water has no enemy).

Relatively cheap oil and a poorly connected public transportation system continue to promote private car use for the middle and upper classes, and the combination of bad roads, frequent flooding, and social ego has boosted the presence of SUVs. Meanwhile, the average, lower-income Lagosian has participated in the proliferation of mini-transport vehicles such as *okadas* (motorcycles) or *danfos* (vans).

Most of Lagos's urban fabric is unplanned, or "informal," the result of an accumulation of communal and privately negotiated spaces, buildings, and micro-infrastructures. The city's growth is so rapid that strategies devised by authorities and city planners become obsolete even before their implementation starts. In

order to promote improvement, the government adopts two scales of intervention: the development of large-scale infrastructure projects, such as highway construction; and the enhancement of smaller-scale road and drainage systems. Meanwhile, inadequate incomes and the uneven distribution of wealth mean the majority of citizens have to set up their own businesses and develop new economies occupying a status somewhere between legal and illegal.

To understand the context of Lagos, we propose two analytical and representational tools: a map and an evidence catalogue. This methodology, based on a quantitative and a qualitative analysis, could be applied to most cities. Our project is then manifested through individual prototype proposals and collectively in three urban views illustrating future visions for the city.

Map and Evidence Catalogue

There are no recent detail maps of Lagos. This may relate to the fact that Lagos is ever changing. So we set ourselves the challenge of developing our own map, with a complexity that is symmetrical to the reality we observed. The search, description, and cataloguing of "evidence" helped us understand both the global and specific contexts. We thus configured an open database that contains examples of the inventions, situations, compromises, and players to be found in Lagos, some endemic, some global, some tangible, some tacit.

Prototypes and Visions

We propose a series of physical and strategic prototypes that enrich the city fabric, learning from its local intelligence and combining with global technologies. These prototypes are manifested as urban visions at a large scale, and as elemental interventions with different functions at a smaller scale. The proposals are visualized in three images depicting a future reality in which the day-to-day skills of "informal" bottom-up initiatives are merged with "formal" top-down plans.

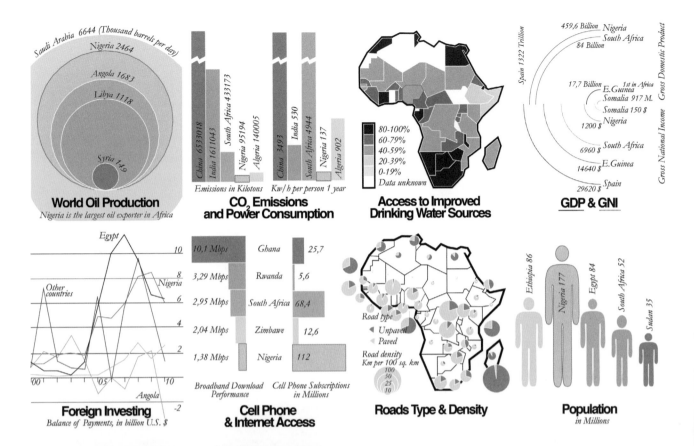

World Oil Production
Nigeria is the largest oil exporter in Africa

Saudi Arabia 6644 *(Thousand barrels per day)*
Nigeria 2464
Angola 1683
Libya 1118
Syria 149

CO₂ Emissions and Power Consumption

Emissions in Kilotons
China 6533018
India 1611043
South Africa 433173
Nigeria 95194
Algeria 140005

Kw/h per person 1 year
China 3493
India 530
South Africa 4944
Nigeria 137
Algeria 902

Access to Improved Drinking Water Sources

80-100%
60-79%
40-59%
20-39%
0-19%
Data unknown

GDP & GNI

Spain 1322 Trillion
459,6 Billion Nigeria
South Africa
84 Billion

17,7 Billion E.Guinea
1st in Africa
Somalia 917 M.
Somalia 150 $
1200 $ Nigeria
6960 $ South Africa
14640 $ E.Guinea
29620 $ Spain

Gross National Income   Gross Domestic Product

Foreign Investing
Balance of Payments, in billion U.S. $

Egypt
Other countries
Nigeria
Angola

'00   '05   '10

10
8
6
4
2
-2

Cell Phone & Internet Access

Broadband Download Performance
10,1 Mbps   Ghana   25,7
3,29 Mbps   Rwanda   5,6
2,95 Mbps   South Africa   68,4
2,04 Mbps   Zimbawe   12,6
1,38 Mbps   Nigeria   112

Cell Phone Subscriptions in Millions

Roads Type & Density

Road type
◄ Unpaved
◄ Paved

Road density
Km per 100 sq. km
100
50
25
10

Population
in Millions

Ethiopia 86
Nigeria 177
Egypt 84
South Africa 52
Sudan 35

The importance of quantitative data cannot be overemphasized: According to a report earlier this year by UN-Habitat, "by 2050, Africa's city dwellers will more than triple, from about 400 million to 1.2 billion— one of the fastest urbanizations in human history." At the same time, the qualitative understanding of a specific city like Lagos, and its social and cultural dynamics within a larger macro-economy, is key to our proposal to bridge local and global issues. As journalist Vivienne Walt has pointed out, "Lagos offers a laboratory for Africa's future."

technologies & materials

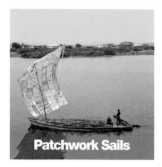 **Patchwork Sails**

 **Water Tower**

 **Keke Marwa**

working communities

 **Cane Craftsmen**

 **Reused Metal Retailers**

 **Art World**

management strategies

 **The Shrine Strategy**

 **Pop-up Strategy**

 **Water Network Strategy**

urban spaces

 **Under the Bridge**

 **Highways**

 **Extreme Billboarding**

human network

 **Chief**

 **Musician**

 **Carpenter**

Generators

LED Façade

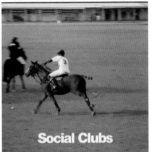

Social Clubs

Sand Miners

Lagos State Strategy

Floweman Strategy

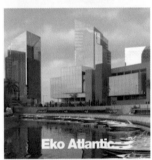

Eko Atlantic

Makoko

Art Dealer

Traffic Jam Seller

Fantasy Masonry

An alternative brick layout to build a wall so it's dynamically permeable. Depending on where you are positioned, it can be opaque or you can see through the brick holes.

Learning from Lagos: A catalogue of evidence, small fragments of reality, describe multiple social, economic, and political layers. These are classified into groups: Technologies & Materials, Working Communities, Management Strategies, Urban Spaces, and Human Network. This evidence is used as a starting point for the design of the prototypes.

OSHODI-ISOLO
AGO PALACE WAY

KILO BUS STOP

MAKOKU

AJEROMI-IFELODU

APAPA
LAGOS HARBOUR

Mapping Lagos Urban Commons: Developing our own Lagos map allows us to understand how our findings relate to the city fabric, mutating and spreading as urban tactics or symbiosis. The project employs tactical urbanism, creating a network of spaces that act as infrastructure for the city, strengthening what already occurs there. Combining large-scale with small-scale urban interventions, these proposals work as catalysts and impact the city at neighborhood and individual scales. The different prototypes are designed to boost, promote, and improve the management of Lagos's urban commons.

LAGOS ISLAND
IKOYI

BANANA ISLAND

ETI OSA
VICTORIA ISLAND

LEKKI

EKO ATLANTIC

LAGOS
urban commons

Energy

The year is 2050, and the abundance or dependence on fossil fuels is history. The city is mainly off-grid. Energy in Lagos is produced from renewable sources and distributed through a decentralized network. Our energy prototypes combine public and private initiatives by transforming former infrastructures. Shimmering solar panel roofs, wind turbines, biomass sources, and clean energy are the order of the day. Thousands of obsolete generator carcasses are recycled into new forms of architecture. Redundant high-tension cable masts are appropriated into urban towers. Health food venues, urban gyms, and extreme sports are popular outlets for social and human energy.

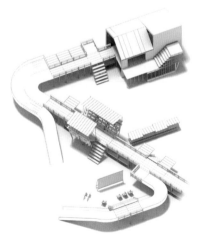

Energy pedagogic center
– Reused generator structure

Social energy infrastructure
– Community workshops

Renewable energy production island
– Viewpoint

Water

The 4th Mainland Bridge has finally established a ring road around Lagos. Congestion in the old city center is so 2008. The new city center—within the ring—is water. It is now just 40 minutes by car from Lekki to Ikeja via Ikorodu, and, better still, just 20 minutes across the city center by speedboat. The city has come to terms with life on water. It is a place where the innovative cultures of Makoko, the grand ambitions of Eko Atlantic City, and the urban characteristics of Venice and Amsterdam all coexist—a truly adapted, resilient, and contemporary African Water City.

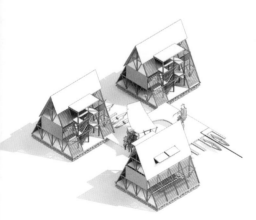

Residential

Recreational

Commercial

Transportation

The means of transportation in the city are highly diverse: cable cars from Falomo, light-rail systems to Badagry, the proposed Alfred Rewane canal, cycling routes, and pedestrian shopping streets provide zones of convergence for all Lagosians.

Existing structures and uses are adapted and connected in new public spaces equipped with self-managed prototypes, such as bus stops and boat docks, street vendor stations, bike repair points, plant vendor shops (or green spaces), and street markets for professionals.

Water local transportation station
– Community storage point

Vehicles repair center
– Go-slow pop-up marketing

Bike repair center
– Local energy production point

TACTICAL URBANISMS: AFRICA

Bicycling Empowerment Network Namibia (BEN Namibia). Bike Ambulance. 2006

Earthship Biotecture. Goderich Waldorf School, Sierra Leone. 2011

Informal access roads in Ard El Lewa, Giza. 2013

Heath Nash. Plastic Bottle Roof Shade, Harare, Zimbabwe. 2011

Azagaia. *O Facebook do Jaimito*. 2011. Ocupações Temporárias, Maputo, Mozambique

Matteo Ferroni. Foroba Yelen: Collective Light for Mali. 2011

Moladi plastic formwork construction system, South Africa. Established 1986

r1. *Hard seat/soft seat*. South Africa. 2013

Nima: Muhinmanchi Art. Imagine Accra Independence Mural Painting, Club Ten, Kanda Highway, Accra. 2011

Swings for Dreams. Play Space, Ratang Bana AIDS Orphanage, Alexandra, South Africa. 2013

Peter Rich Architects. Thulumtwana Children's Facility, Gauteng, South Africa. 2000

Violence Prevention through Urban Upgrading (VPUU). Active Box, Khayelitsha, Cape Town. 2006

SEED. Rocklands Urban Abundance Center, Cape Town. 2011

For more information:
http://unevengrowth.moma.org

URBZ: user-generated cities, Mumbai
Ensamble Studio/MIT-POPlab, Madrid and Cambridge

How can urbanists, architects, community groups, and end users come together to produce ever-evolving, dynamic, urban habitats? We explore paths that are both conflict-ridden and full of potential.

Mumbai beyond the slum and the high-rise

Mumbai is a city of disparate and incoherent habitats, loosely tied into a restless, shape-shifting whole. It emerged through various historical encounters—from the marshy margins of medieval kingdoms to expansive Portuguese colonial landscapes, and from a constrained English port city to its latest identity as a global metropolis—to become the dense and intense city we know today. Mumbai continues to evade attempts to reshape it into a modern, standardized metropolis.

Contemporary Mumbai is represented in bipolar terms as a city of slums and high-rises. In reality, its great diversity of built-forms represents creative ways in which inhabitants occupy urban space. Dharavi and Shivaji Nagar, officially treated as slums, have grown incrementally over time and embody many complex dynamics with their own spatial innovations and organizational strategies. They are part of a larger urban fabric of similar neighborhoods that reportedly absorbs well over half of the metropolis's 12 million residents.

These neighborhoods are composed of hundreds and thousands of tiny homes squeezed into a disproportionately small share of the city's land. The homes exist in large interconnected collectives and often serve as both residences and workspaces. What we call "tool-house" is a distinctive housing archetype across Asia. It combines and compresses various functions. Its other avatars include Singapore's shop-house and Tokyo's home-factory. These efficient live-work spaces exist all around the world, independent of geographies and classes.

In Mumbai, the tool-house, which generates value through its use rather than land speculation, is the lifeline that keeps millions of people afloat and allows them to grow roots and a future in the city. Many poor artisanal communities, manual workers, and small-time traders—often from castes historically belonging to the so-called low strata—productively occupy these spaces. In the name of redevelopment, however, these neighborhoods are progressively being replaced

appears as new territory to claim, where live-work conditions and public infrastructures recover their rightful place, thus liberating the excessive pressure on the land. Through design, the existing incompatibility between typology and scale gets diluted, the productive hybridization of different uses—inherent to the spirit of the place—is reinforced, and new alternatives to single-minded redevelopment strategies become refreshed.

Out of a creative and sometimes troubled collaboration, the in situ work of URBZ and the inventive explorations of Ensamble Studio/MIT-POPlab draw from a collage of tactics, technologies, visions, and imaginations. They prevent an automatic disqualification of homegrown neighborhoods to present them not as tabula rasa but as a "tabula pronta" with real value to drive any development strategy.

In the end, it is the users themselves who will make the final difference by seizing the tools of institutions and experts to continue doing what they have always done—to control and shape their environments with higher levels of professionalism and good sense. Never before have creative collaborations between planners, architects, local groups, and end users been at once so conflict ridden and full of potential. Unleashing this potential requires overcoming narrow interests and miscommunication.

What we envision here is not a speculative future, but an expanded present, where inhabitants can at last reclaim growth for themselves. Cities would be substantially different if their processes of urbanization could align with these goals. It is time for radical, incremental strategies that align global experiences with local knowledge and experience of urban spaces.

by single-function high-rise residential blocks, revealing the arrested imagination of the authorities.

Instead of feeling threatened by a planet of slums in need of clearance, we believe in a planet of neighborhoods and habitats in different stages of evolution. Taking such a view, we can do greater justice to those living in habitats that have gradually developed over time thanks to the efforts

of their residents. This will help reclaim the idea of growth in ways that escape old-fashioned notions of urban development to pave the way for richer and more diverse environments shaped by users' needs and aspirations.

Imagining how growth could happen in such dense and use-intensive environments, we explore new technologies and territories. The air

Planet of Slums?: One way to appreciate the potential of homegrown neighborhoods is to acknowledge them as a universal reality. The "mashup" collages shown here provocatively mix Dharavi with streets in São Paulo, Tokyo, and Perugia, Italy. They express the propensity of users in diverse cities to incrementally improve and shape their habitats to produce vibrant and functional neighborhoods.

Arrested Development or Homegrown Neighborhoods?: Communities, such as those shown below, have relied on in-house building skills for a long time. These homegrown neighborhoods persist in spite of heavy odds: authorities and professional builders, responding to a speculation-fueled real estate market, often prefer to raze them to build inexpensive mass housing. By granting these neighborhoods the security of tenure and recognizing them as legitimate spaces, they might be transformed into quality habitats.

The Tool House
Living and working in Mumbai

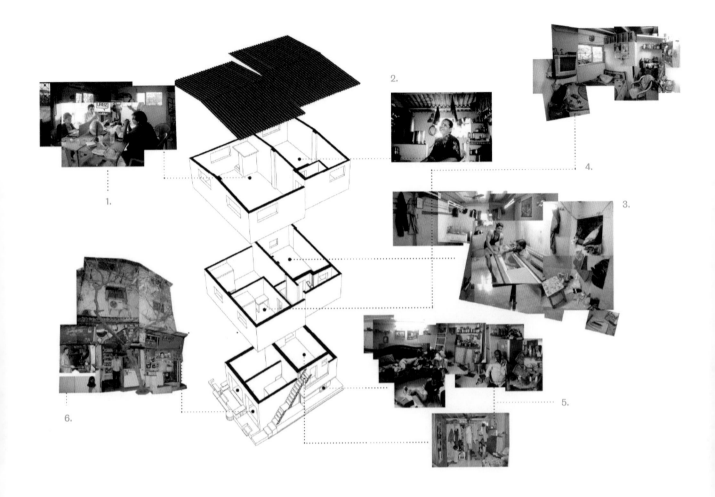

1.

6.

2.

4.

3.

5.

Growing Homes: The tool house is typical of the residence-cum-workspace found in homegrown neighborhoods in Mumbai and other Asian cities. Derived from the artisan's or trader's home, it operates counter to today's excessively zoned and planned urban norm. If rebooted and validated, it can revitalize urban spaces by distributing resources more evenly and by improving local infrastructure.

1. Office: Over five years, URBZ added a toilet, insulated the roof, and changed windows.

2. Rental: After moving from place to place when the industrial mills shut down, Sanganamma finally found a sense of belonging in Dharavi.

3. Workshop: Mohammad and Jaium work as embroiderers by day and sleep here with their coworkers at night. This arrangement increases their savings, which they send back home.

4. Rental: Tenants Malar and her daughter, Jaffia, feel secure in this house, though the father is away in Africa for most of the year.

5. Dwelling: The Raphaels family are the first occupants of this tiny plot, provided by the government in 1983 as part of a resettlement scheme.

6. Shop: Raza has run this ice cream shop for five years, sharing it with the Raphaelses' mobile shop.

Reclaim Growth: The office below
represents the typical life cycle
of a homegrown structure. Located
in the suburban neighborhood of
Govandi, Shivaji Nagar is one of the
most marginalized areas of Mumbai,
and municipal authorities destroyed
it once it grew above the legally
permitted height of 14 feet. It was
then rebuilt with lightweight material.

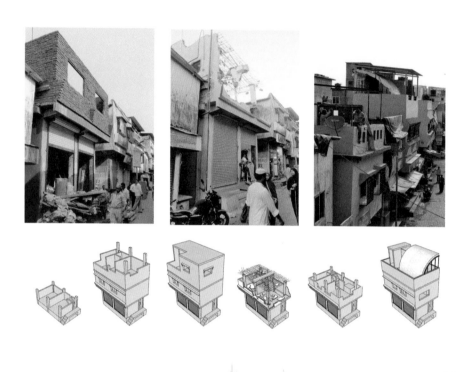

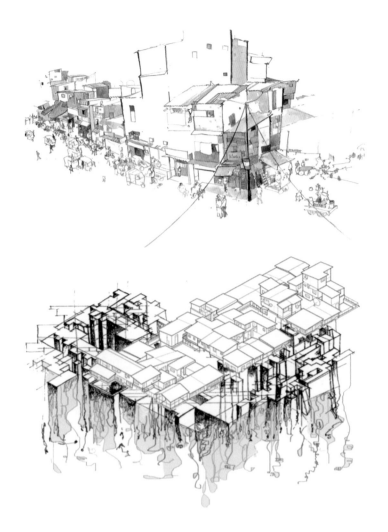

URBZ, together with the builder of their office, the architects sP+a and the engineering firm Arup, continues to evolve pragmatic responses to affordable housing needs following the homegrown template. The drawings above served as the basis for a project currently in construction. At left, an artist responds to the project by conjuring a vision of its many possibilities.

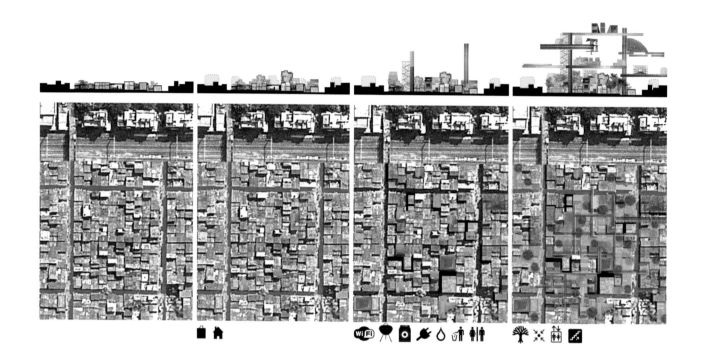

Ultra-Light Growth: The instability of the ground, the need for spatial flexibility, and the insecurity of tenancy make the idea of growing light—technically, functionally, and conceptually—suitable for homegrown neighborhoods. Ensamble Studio/MIT-POPlab's ultra-light construction systems, right, can be applied to build second and third levels in preexisting structures. Easily appropriated with available tools and materials, these ultra-light systems can be assembled and disassembled without incurring great costs or effort.

Supragrowth: Reacting to the lack of public services and the dispirited character of existing urban "rehabilitation strategies," Ensamble Studio/MIT-POPlab proposes Supraextructures as a way to reclaim the air for even growth. Supraextructures are three-dimensional infrastructures that touch the ground punctually to connect to other networks; build new "flying carpet" levels for city expansion that prevent the indifferent deletion of preexisting fabrics; facilitate productive balances between public and private realms; and service old and new residents. Learning from the homegrown neighborhoods at the ground, they enable incremental growth in the air, integrating different architectures, scales, and, foremost, people.

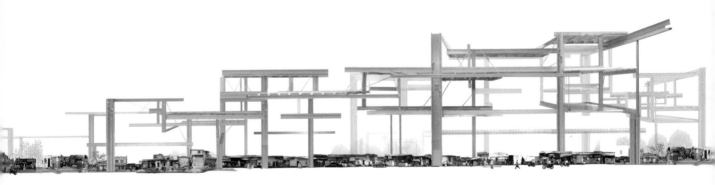

Tabula Pronta: Ultra-light growth and supragrowth reinforce the idea that homegrown neighborhoods are fertile grounds to work with—they have the dynamism and flexibility to absorb different urban tensions and can organically coexist with new urban forms. With this understanding as the collaborative basis for the different agents constructing the city, there is great potential for the creation of diverse urban conditions. Instead of building a flattening future that erases the past and the present, we propose expanding the present.

URBZ: user-generated cities & Ensamble Studio/MIT-POPlab

TACTICAL URBANISMS: SOUTH ASIA

Abin Chaudhuri and Tilak Ajmera of Abin Design Studio. Rainbow Field, Kolkata. 2014

Akshay Sharma. LaXmi, board game, Rajasthan, India. 2013

Bakul Foundation. My Tree Campaign, Bhubaneshwar, India. 2008

Caltech and the Kohler Company with ODDS (Open Door Design Studio). Mobile restroom, New Delhi. 2012

Dabbawalla lunch box delivery in Mumbai. 2009

S.N. Bhobe for the Mumbai
Metropolitan Region Development
Authority (MMRDA). Bandra Skywalk,
Mumbai. 2008

Maha Kumbh Mela, Allahabad, India.
2013

Spontaneous Architecture at the Bezalel
Academy (SABA). Children's Corner at
the Center for Rural Knowledge, Gujarat,
India. 2012

Urfunlab Surat. Storm Water Pipes,
Surat, India. 2010

Filipe Balestra and Sara Göransson of
Urban Nouveau. Incremental Housing,
Pune, India. 2009

Wello and Catapult Design. WaterWheel,
India. 2011

For more information:
http://unevengrowth.moma.org

SITU Studio, New York
Cohabitation Strategies (CohStra), Rotterdam and New York

Supporting the thriving growth of a luxury megacity, there is an invisible New York in which a substantial population struggles to afford their homes, concealing the breadth of unevenness that permeates the city.

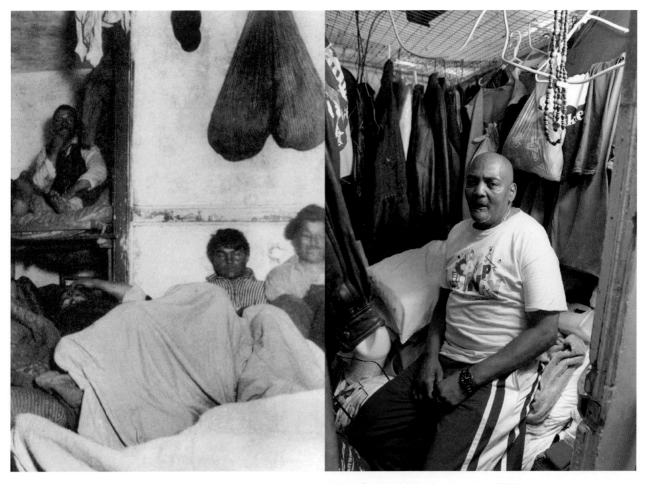

From left: Jacob August Riis. *Lodgers in Bayard Street Tenement, Five Cents a Spot* (detail). 1889. Gelatin silver print, printed 1957, 6 9/16" × 4 ¾" (15.7 × 12 cm). The Museum of Modern Art, New York. Gift of the Museum of the City of New York; Michael Fidler, 66, originally from Brooklyn, has been living in the Sun Bright Hotel at 140 Hester Street for eleven years; the accommodations measure 7 by 5 feet. 2013

Over the past two decades, policies at all government levels, as well as global investment and profit-driven development, have dominated the city's growth and engineered its social divide. With middle-income households in decline, New York's rapid growth manifests in its trans-formed neighborhoods and luxury developments. The city's uneven expansion of wealth has resulted in a marked scarcity of housing, pushing poor and middle-income New Yorkers into increasingly cramped and expen-sive living conditions.

With average monthly market rents exceeding $3,000, and a median household income that barely reaches $51,000 per year, more than half of all renter households are rent burdened—nearly one-third spend at least half of their income on housing. Deregulation of private rental hous-ing, withdrawal of funds for rental subsidies, disinvestment in housing provision for the poor, and stagnation of wages have made it increasingly difficult for more than half of the population to afford to live in the city, and have contributed to an unprece-dented number of homeless people. Nearly 55,000 people sleep at night in the municipal shelter system, of whom 23,000 are children.

A lesser-known consequence of the affordability crisis is that large segments of the New York population have been forced into informal rental markets, a condition that is at once pervasive and hidden. One simply scratches the surface to find the varied informal financial, social, and spatial networks that are sustained in the shadows of New York City's legal frameworks. The scale of the cash-based economies, strained infrastructure, and illegally converted dwellings are evidence of how many New Yorkers are poor and often con-cealed from view.

These informal markets have carved up and now occupy the interiors of endless rows of apart-ment buildings, town houses, and

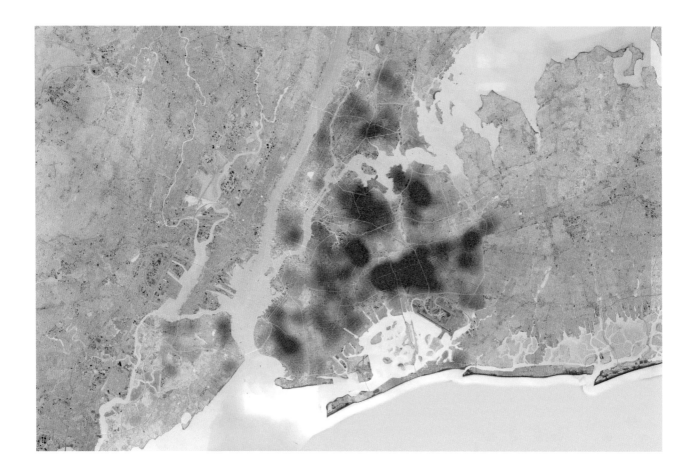

high-rises, forming a network of emergent typologies that have adapted, subdivided, or converted existing spaces to accommodate the growing number of those who cannot find a place within the formal housing market. This population works in the lowest paid jobs. Most are employed in the service sectors that keep this so-called "luxury city" upright and thriving. This underlines how the quality of life to which so many New Yorkers have become accustomed relies upon the services provided by so many whose presence is rarely acknowledged or discussed. More than a century ago, in what we like to believe was a different New York, Jacob Riis identified this same injustice: citizens become invisible within existing housing stock and are left out of the discussions, policies,

and design decisions that shape the city in which they live.

Given these circumstances, two alternative approaches address the crisis of affordability in New York.

Cohabitation Strategies proposes the development of Housing Cooperative Trusts across the city through a hybrid tenure framework. This model challenges the traditional conception of property, including management and ownership. Land and buildings are not fully owned by city authorities, nonprofits, community stakeholders, or tenants, but by all of them collectively. This scalable scheme aspires to guarantee permanent affordable living and working spaces while defining the relations required to build social equity and sustain future generations.

SITU Studio proposes a scenario where underutilized urban spaces could be opened up to a new type of incremental growth that is facilitated through neighborhood-based organizations called Community Growth Corporations. By benefiting from high-density development in adjacent urban centers, outer-borough neighborhoods would collectively finance community-wide improvements that would provide access to rooftops, backyards, and other occupiable spaces, cultivating incremental density within existing fabric. Facilitated by a unique mixed-income connective building typology, a new informal rooftop urbanism could emerge in a city with scarce remaining land.

This map, which shows illegal conversions as reported to the New York City Department of Buildings, reveals "hot spots" concentrated in the more remote sections of Queens, Brooklyn, and the Bronx where large numbers of recent immigrants live. By definition a difficult condition to quantify, this data presents a notional geography of New York's informal housing market.

Three public workshops organized with participants from New York City's art, architecture, urban planning, and housing disciplines and a documentary, *Uneven Growth: Revealing the Other New York City*, were developed as research tools to reveal the consequences of the predatory housing crisis.

Housing is both, a use-value and exchange-value...The exchange value system has failed, it has failed miserably.

We have seen a shift in policies that caters to private developers and how much money can be made on the use of land as opposed to using land for the benefit of people.

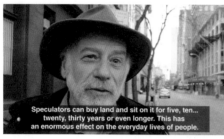

Speculators can buy land and sit on it for five, ten... twenty, thirty years or even longer. This has an enormous effect on the everyday lives of people.

New York City is a remarkable place, unfortunately a dramatically unequal one...a large amount of people does not make near to afford the cost of housing.

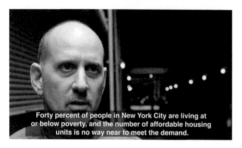

Forty percent of people in New York City are living at or below poverty, and the number of affordable housing units is no way near to meet the demand.

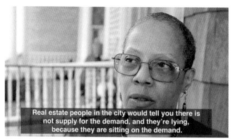

Real estate people in the city would tell you there is not supply for the demand, and they're lying, because they are sitting on the demand.

Your landlord is probably not your landlord, but a financial institution, equity firm, or hedge fund. Your apartment is just a number on a spreadsheet.

The foreclosure crisis is disproportionately affecting people of color, women and children...and the middle class, especially the black and Latino middle class.

You can walk down any street in New York...and there is a homeless person on a bench right next to a guy that is running a multibillion dollar corporation.

Three times more vacant spaces in New York City than there are homeless people.

Stills from *Uneven Growth: Revealing the Other New York City*, clockwise from upper left: David Harvey, CUNY; Rachel LaForest, Right to the City Alliance; Brad Lander, member of the NYC Council; Kendall Jackman, Picture the Homeless and New York City Community Land Initiative; Rachel Falcone and Michael Premo, Sandy Storyline and Housing Is a Human Right projects; Frank Morales, Episcopal priest, writer, and housing activist; Rob Robinson, Take Back the Land National Movement; Laura Gottesdiener, journalist and author; Harvey Epstein, Urban Justice Center; Tom Angotti, Hunter College and CUNY.

BEDROOM1
110 ft²

BEDROOM2
110 ft²

BEDROOM3
100 ft²

BEDROOM4
85 ft²

750 ft² $ 1250

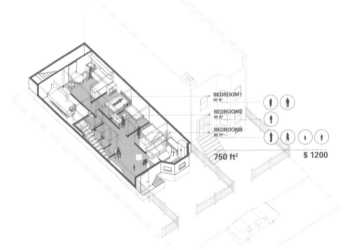

BEDROOM1
85 ft²

BEDROOM2
85 ft²

BEDROOM3
85 ft²

750 ft² $ 1200

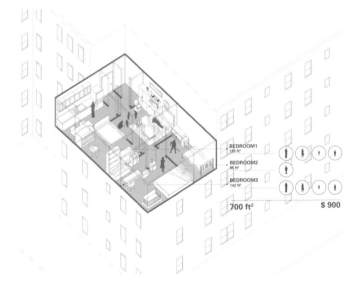

BEDROOM1
133 ft²

BEDROOM2
95 ft²

BEDROOM3
142 ft²

700 ft² $ 900

As many as 200,000 illegally converted apartments exist in New York City. Interiors of existing units as well as cellars, attics, and industrial spaces are subdivided into smaller spaces to accommodate this hidden density. Photographs from site visits and virtual reconstructions of emblematic apartment interiors render visible this hidden New York. While accommodating the city's growing population at affordable rates, the informal nature of this market prevents tenants from claiming basic housing rights.

To counteract the current housing crisis, CohStra developed a new framework to rehabilitate industrial structures, multifamily buildings, and clusters of two- and three-family homes and to establish new construction on vacant and underutilized lots.

The proposed Housing Cooperative Trusts, shown below, comprise four components: a community district land trust, a mutual housing association, a cooperative housing trust, and a district-based credit union.

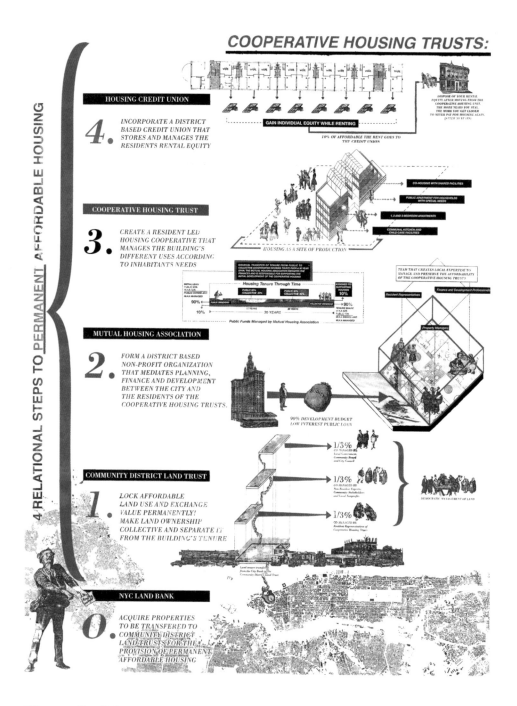

COOPERATIVE HOUSING TRUSTS:

4. RELATIONAL STEPS TO PERMANENT AFFORDABLE HOUSING

HOUSING CREDIT UNION

4. INCORPORATE A DISTRICT BASED CREDIT UNION THAT STORES AND MANAGES THE RESIDENTS RENTAL EQUITY

GAIN INDIVIDUAL EQUITY WHILE RENTING

10% OF AFFORDABLE THE RENT GOES TO THE CREDIT UNION

DISPOSE OF YOUR RENTAL EQUITY AFTER MOVING FROM THE COOPERATIVE HOUSING UNIT. THE MORE YEARS YOU STAY, THE MORE YOU GET CLOSER TO NEVER PAY FOR HOUSING AGAIN. (AFTER 30 YEARS)

COOPERATIVE HOUSING TRUST

3. CREATE A RESIDENT LED HOUSING COOPERATIVE THAT MANAGES THE BUILDING'S DIFFERENT USES ACCORDING TO INHABITANTS NEEDS

CO-HOUSING WITH SHARED FACILITIES
PUBLIC APARTMENT FOR HOUSEHOLDS WITH SPECIAL NEEDS
1, 2 AND 3 BEDROOM APARTMENTS
COMMUNAL KITCHEN AND CHILD CARE FACILITIES

HOUSING AS A SITE OF PRODUCTION

GRADUAL TRANSFER OF TENURE FROM PUBLIC TO COLLECTIVE COOPERATIVE HOUSING TRUSTS OVER A 30 YEAR SPAN. THE MUTUAL HOUSING ASSOCIATION MEDIATES THE FINANCES AND IS RESPONSIBLE FOR SUPPORTING THE INITIAL DEVELOPMENT OF THE COOPERATIVE HOUSING

Housing Tenure Through Time

INITIAL LOAN
90%
10%
PUBLIC 90%
COLLECTIVE 10%
PUBLIC 10%
COLLECTIVE 90%
ASSIGNED TO SUPPORTING HOUSING 10%
90%

10 YEARS   30 YEARS

Public Funds Managed by Mutual Housing Association

TEAM THAT CREATES LOCAL EXPERTISE TO MANAGE AND PRESERVE THE AFFORDABILITY OF THE COOPERATIVE HOUSING TRUSTS
Resident Representatives
Finance and Development Professionals
Property Managers

MUTUAL HOUSING ASSOCIATION

2. FORM A DISTRICT BASED NON-PROFIT ORGANIZATION THAT MEDIATES PLANNING, FINANCE AND DEVELOPMENT BETWEEN THE CITY AND THE RESIDENTS OF THE COOPERATIVE HOUSING TRUSTS.

90% DEVELOPMENT BUDGET LOW INTEREST PUBLIC LOAN

1/3% CO-MANAGED BY Local Government, Community Board and City Council

1/3% CO-MANAGED BY Non-Resident Experts, Community Stakeholders and Local Nonprofits

1/3% CO-MANAGED BY Resident Representatives of Cooperative Housing Trust

DEMOCRATIC MANAGEMENT OF LAND

COMMUNITY DISTRICT LAND TRUST

1. LOCK AFFORDABLE LAND USE AND EXCHANGE VALUE PERMANENTLY! MAKE LAND OWNERSHIP COLLECTIVE AND SEPARATE IT FROM THE BUILDING'S TENURE

Land tenure transferred from the City Bank to the Community District Land Trust

NYC LAND BANK

0. ACQUIRE PROPERTIES TO BE TRANSFERED TO COMMUNITY DISTRICT LAND TRUSTS FOR THE PROVISION OF PERMANENT AFFORDABLE HOUSING

SITU's proposed Community Growth Corporation (CGC), shown below, is premised on a public auction system that monetizes the unused excess buildable square footage of affordable housing properties in exchange for shares in the CGC. Held in trust for the benefit of income-restricted residents, capital from CGC shares is used to develop and preserve mixed-income housing. Financial returns are used for physical improvements and for community investments that are subject to the participatory governance of this crowd-sourced investment vehicle.

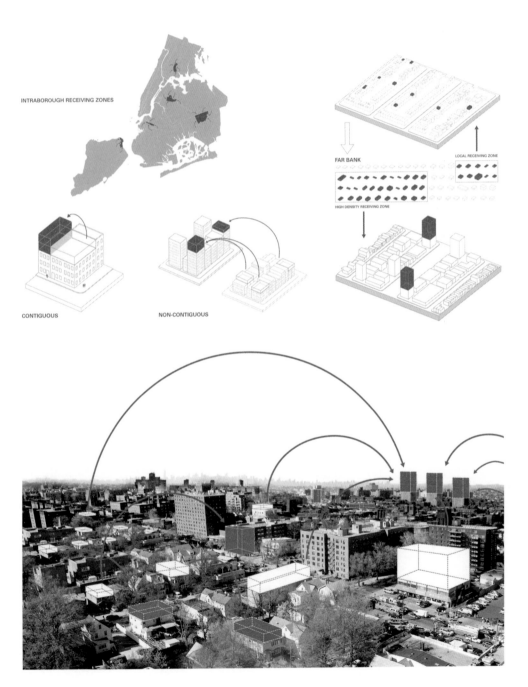

Public resources traditionally have gone either to the government for the provision and administration of housing or to private entities for the production and commercialization of dwellings. CohStra's proposed Housing Cooperative Trusts challenge this convention by delegating power and resources from the public to the collective.

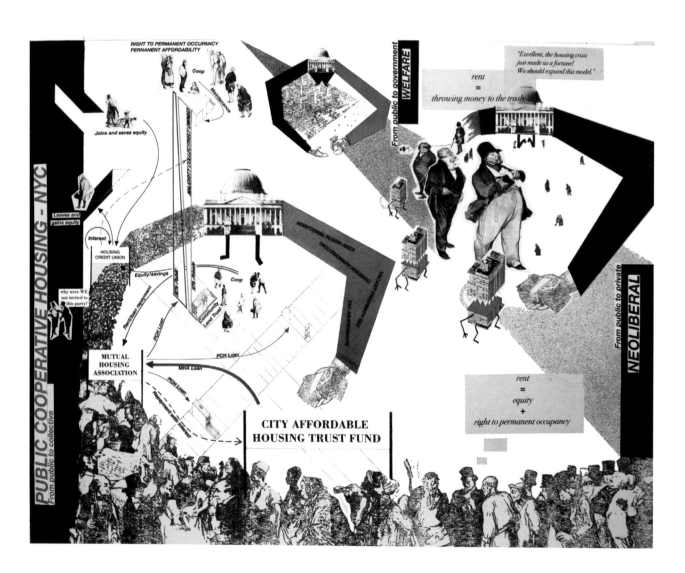

This dwelling scheme accommodates nontraditional units, such as cohousing and shared facilities, and associates permanent affordable living units with learning and working spaces to make housing a site of production.

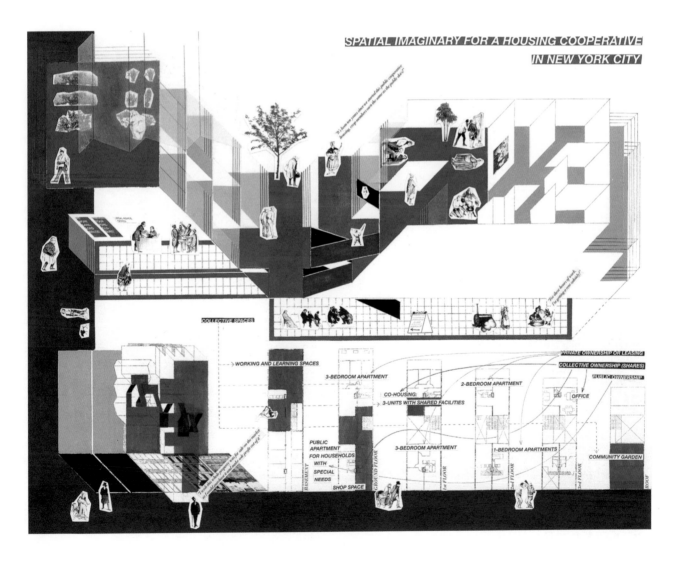

SPATIAL IMAGINARY FOR A HOUSING COOPERATIVE IN NEW YORK CITY

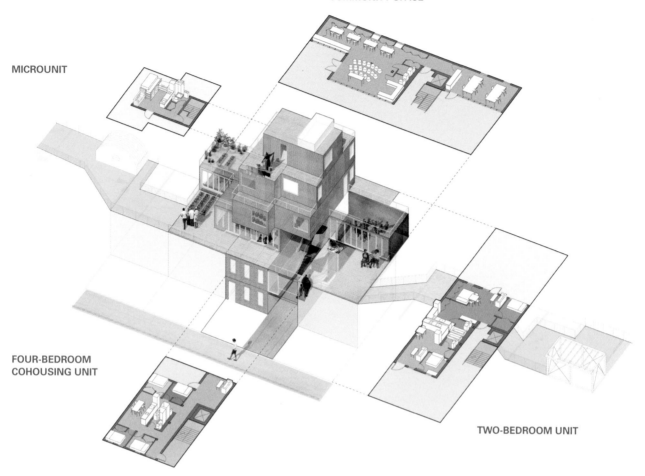

COMMUNITY SPACE

MICROUNIT

FOUR-BEDROOM COHOUSING UNIT

TWO-BEDROOM UNIT

Above, a novel form of mixed-use, mixed-income urbanism developed by the local CGC links the public street to a new roofscape. Mid-rise developments at one roof level are anchored by a community facility at the adjacent roof level, providing long-term affordable housing that can be tailored to the demographics of each neighborhood and access to new, elevated public spaces. The tactical nature of this roofscape within the existing urban fabric inspires "home-grown" additions and propels a new mode of incremental growth.

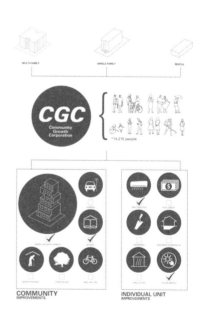

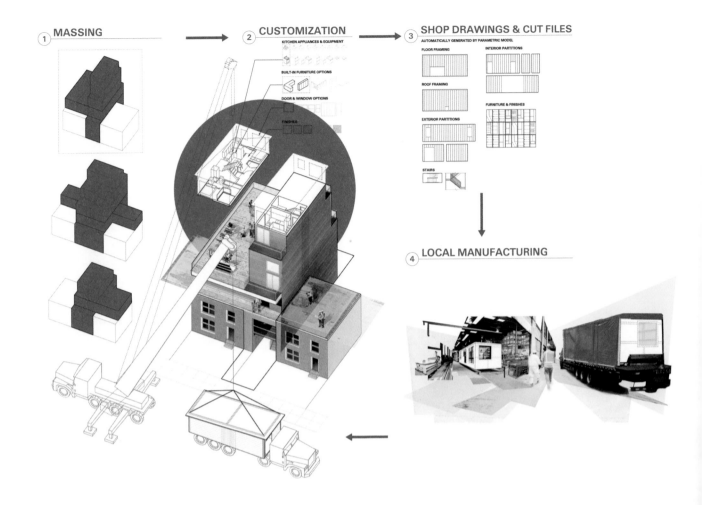

1 MASSING

2 CUSTOMIZATION

KITCHEN APPLIANCES & EQUIPMENT

BUILT-IN FURNITURE OPTIONS

DOOR & WINDOW OPTIONS

FINISHES

3 SHOP DRAWINGS & CUT FILES

AUTOMATICALLY GENERATED BY PARAMETRIC MODEL

FLOOR FRAMING

INTERIOR PARTITIONS

ROOF FRAMING

FURNITURE & FINISHES

EXTERIOR PARTITIONS

STAIRS

4 LOCAL MANUFACTURING

New York City has one of the highest costs of construction in the country. These costs can be mitigated by combining modular construction with advances in Building Information Modeling (BIM). For the proposed roofscape typology, a streamlined approach to design and construction allows for its inexpensive customization to different neighborhoods: a series of virtual parametric modular platforms tie site-specific design parameters directly into factory assembly methodologies, permitting a new homegrown industry of modular construction.

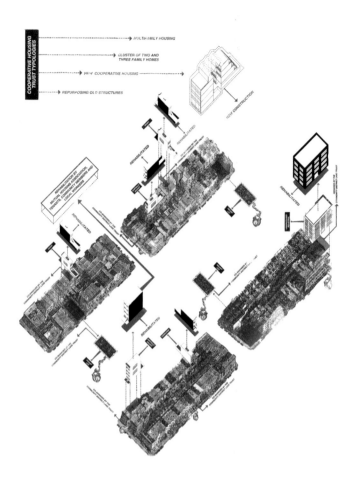

In a typical low-rise residential district of northern Queens, top right, the city is envisioned as the manifestation of an incremental, community-driven growth. CohStra's Housing Cooperative Trusts and SITU's Community Growth Corporation are combined to populate the neighborhood with long-term affordable housing, public services, and community spaces while preserving the urban fabric that makes the neighborhood unique.

CGC-facilitated community improvements include
new multi-modal street hubs, and a variety of green
spaces such as rooftop farms and public parks.

TACTICAL URBANISMS: NORTH AMERICA

envelope A+D. NOW_Hunters Point, Bayview-Hunters Point, San Francisco. 2013

Depave. Depavers at Lewis Elementary School, Portland, Oregon. 2011

Interboro Partners. LentSpace, New York. 2009

Macro Sea. Summer Streets dumpster pool, New York. 2010

Mark Reigelman II. The Reading Nest, Cleveland Public Library, Cleveland. 2013

Michael Rakowitz. *Joe Heywood's paraSITE shelter,* Battery Park City, Manhattan. 2000

SLO Architecture. Harvest Dome,
New York. 2013

UNSTABLE (Marcos Zotes). Your Text
Here, Detroit. 2012

New York City Department of
Transportation (NYC DOT). Green Light
for Midtown, Columbus Circle, New York.
2009

Rural Studio, Auburn University. Lions
Park Playscape, Greensboro, Alabama.
2010

New Orleans Airlift. The Music Box, New
Orleans. 2011–12

Rebar and Reuben Margolin. ParkCycle,
San Francisco. 2007

International Design Clinic.
chainlinkGREEN, Philadelphia. 2009

Pavement to Parks Program. 3876
Noriega Street Parklet, San Francisco.
2012

For more information:
http://unevengrowth.moma.org

**RUA Arquitetos,
Rio de Janeiro
MAS Urban Design,
ETH Zurich**

Common in tropical climates, *varandas* reflect the Brazilian way of life. They provide the inspiration for a catalogue of consumer goods that promotes the making of the city as a collective endeavor bringing together diverse social milieus.

Morro do Alemão, Rio de Janeiro. 2012

A survey of Rio de Janeiro's contrasting urban landscape ultimately reveals unevenness as a dominant feature of the city. While extreme topography constantly confronts the city with nature, the uneven growth patterns of a fragmented urban landscape are explicitly articulated in the contrast between rich and poor, between *asfalto* and *morro* (official city and favelas). The visibility and obvious presence of the favelas stand for the failure of urban planning and the inability to manage the city in an even way, but it also shows the consequences of self-organization, of an urban production made by the people.

Rio de Janeiro can be considered exemplary of Brazil's reputation as one of the world's most unequal nation states. However, if we look at the nation's income distribution, things have drastically changed in the last decade. Due to increased social mobility, big portions of the lower class can now be considered middle class—during the last seven years, the Brazilian lower middle class has increased by 40 million people and currently represents the largest segment of the population. In Rio de Janeiro, 60 percent of favela residents now belong to this emerging middle class.

If Brazil is to become a middle-class country, does this also mean that unevenness is decreasing? The protesters that are currently shaking the country are claiming that the opposite is the case: in view of the investments at stake for the realization of mega-events such as the FIFA World Cup or the upcoming Olympic Games, the equal distribution of public services and educational facilities remains an unfulfilled promise. As a matter of fact, the discontent of large parts of the population clearly expresses the gap between the aspirations of an emerging consumer class and the lack of urban equality.

While redistribution of resources and proper investment in infrastructure remain valid claims for undoing inequalities, the question is whether governmental action is capable of resolving the problem while operating within an economic system that is increasingly transforming the city

into a setting for market-driven development dependent upon corporate protection.

In view of the dominance of market models, what kind of tactic can be deployed to allow an urban production that responds to the needs of the people beyond the standardized solutions of the prevalent urban economy? What is more, how can the emerging middle class become a mediator between segregated worlds as well as find its own way of life beyond the aspirations of a globalized consumer culture? What if the market could offer commodities that enable the users to reappropriate the urban environment in a more sustainable way by promoting the existing qualities of Brazilian street life?

In the face of everyday challenges, the *cariocas* (inhabitants of Rio) have always found ways to appropriate and subvert prevalent systems, which become explicit in the cultural phenomenon and the tactic of the *puxadinho*. Found all over Rio, *puxadinhos* are add-ons to existing structures, typical in Rio's self-built environments, that are created by people with minimal means from leftover and recycled materials. Operating as extensions beyond the boundaries of private property, *puxadinhos* collectively transform the built environment, incorporating and embracing new qualities and uses.

Inspired by the *puxadinho*, *Varanda Products* accommodate the logic of the market in order to transform it. Serving as transitional spaces between inside and outside, *varandas* are architectural elements that are simultaneously domestic and public, creating an ambiguous condition that is open to multiple uses. The *varanda* operates as interface between individual and community; it offers places for encounters among various social groups; and it provides the middle ground that opens space for negotiation, gathering, and play. *Varanda Products* are tailored to create opportunities for social interaction in the urban environment.

The *Varanda Products* line relinks urban goods and their uses in everyday life—it offers consumer products addressed at diverse social milieus so as to bring them together. The spread of *Varanda Products* is dispersed but insinuates itself everywhere by encouraging small-scale entrepreneurship. *Varanda Products* activate the desire to remake the city with the openness and playfulness that is typical of the *carioca* way of life.

Zooming out from Rio de Janeiro's postcard view another reality appears: the contrast between the rich and the poor as expressed in the confrontation of _asfalto_ and _morro_—the city built on asphalt and the city that grew informally in the hills. Yet in Rio's new economy, formerly excluded areas like the favelas play an increasingly significant role. As real estate prices skyrocket, large portions of the lower middle class are now housed within the favelas—representing newly emergent consumers and a target for further market expansion.

EU SÓ VENDO A VISTA

"Es só vendo a vista" quotes an artwork by Marcos Chaves and can be translated in two ways: "I'm only selling the view," or "I only accept cash."

João recently added a veranda to his workshop, where he repairs and resells ventilators. The veranda quickly became a meeting place for the neighbors to have a beer and chat after work. João now plans to transform the roof into a terrace for gatherings and barbecues with friends. In Rio, informal extensions are called _puxadinhos_; they reflect a typical way _cariocas_ appropriate and subvert existing spaces.

Minha casa, meu puxadinho!

"Minha casa, meu puxadinho" refers to the Brazilian government's program for mass housing, "Minha Casa, Minha Vida" (My House, My Life).

As a counter-model to the self-built city, the gated condominiums where João works as a doorman represent a lifestyle to which many people aspire. Yet the generic architecture of these privatized enclaves does not leave much space for local cultures. Designed largely to meet real estate interests, they promote exclusiveness and social segregation. João is looking at an advertisement promoting new products: "Varanda Products—The Carioca Way of City Making!"

Varanda Products
The Carioca Way of City-Making
Good for You
Good for the City

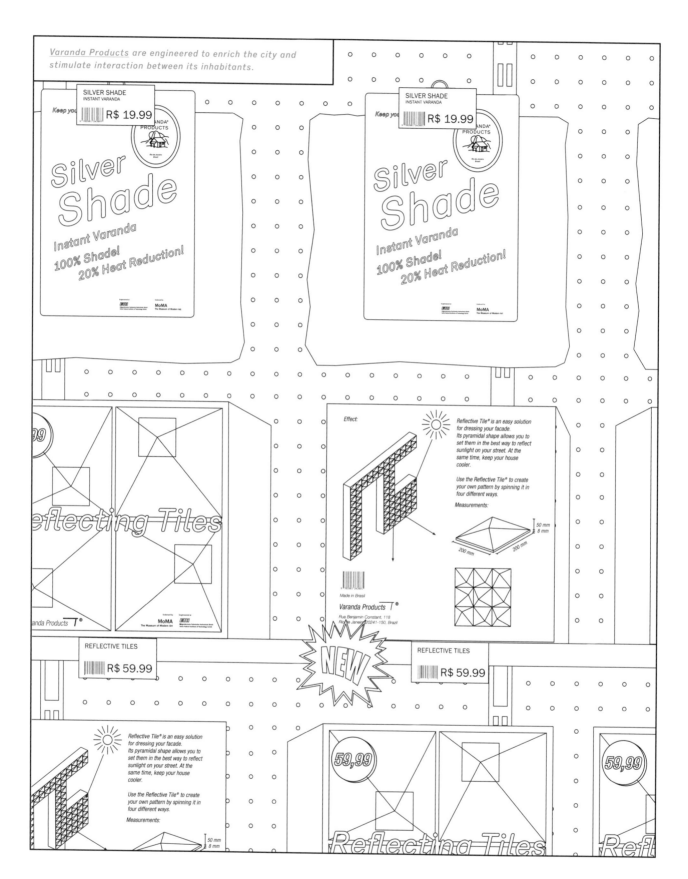

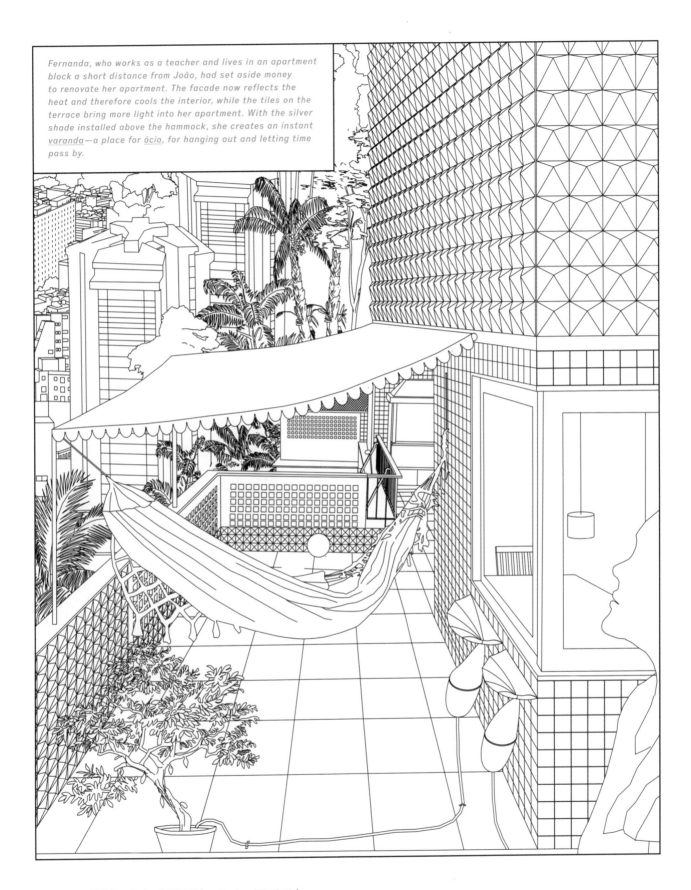

Fernanda, who works as a teacher and lives in an apartment block a short distance from João, had set aside money to renovate her apartment. The facade now reflects the heat and therefore cools the interior, while the tiles on the terrace bring more light into her apartment. With the silver shade installed above the hammock, she creates an instant *varanda*—a place for *ócio*, for hanging out and letting time pass by.

Varanda Products are being replicated across diverse neighborhoods: Covered walkways and escalators connect outdoor spaces. Water collectors and reservoirs provide sustainable local water supplies. Implementation of these new urban goods ranges from the domestic to the urban scale, bridging a once prevalent spatial divide and promoting the coexistence of diverse social milieus.

RUA Arquitetos & MAS Urban Design, ETH Zurich

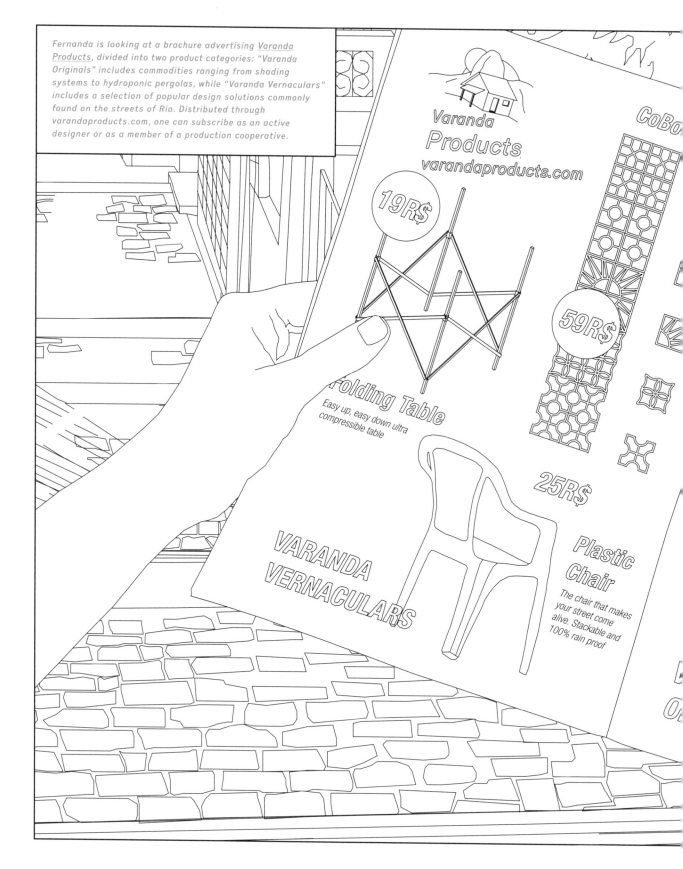

Fernanda is looking at a brochure advertising <u>Varanda Products</u>, divided into two product categories: "Varanda Originals" includes commodities ranging from shading systems to hydroponic pergolas, while "Varanda Vernaculars" includes a selection of popular design solutions commonly found on the streets of Rio. Distributed through varandaproducts.com, one can subscribe as an active designer or as a member of a production cooperative.

Varanda
Products
varandaproducts.com

CoBo

19R$

59R$

Folding Table
Easy up, easy down ultra compressible table

25R$

VARANDA VERNACULARS

Plastic Chair
The chair that makes your street come alive. Stackable and 100% rain proof

Papaya Umbrella

Silver Shade!

Silver Shade! ® is an easy solution to create nice outdoor spaces in no time. Simply use a rope or a beam to hook up the shade between buildings, poles or alleys.

The special Silver Shade! ® coating keeps the shaded space 20% cooler than Blue Shade or other fabric cooling devices by reflecting 60% of sunlight directly back into the atmosphere.

Effect:

60% Reflection

149R$

different ns in stock. tion that od

er to collect, filter and water equipped with hoses howers. Consists of a vertical ollector, metal rods and cover.

neighborhoods and an create a great d responsible space!

NDA NALS

Silver Shade

19R$

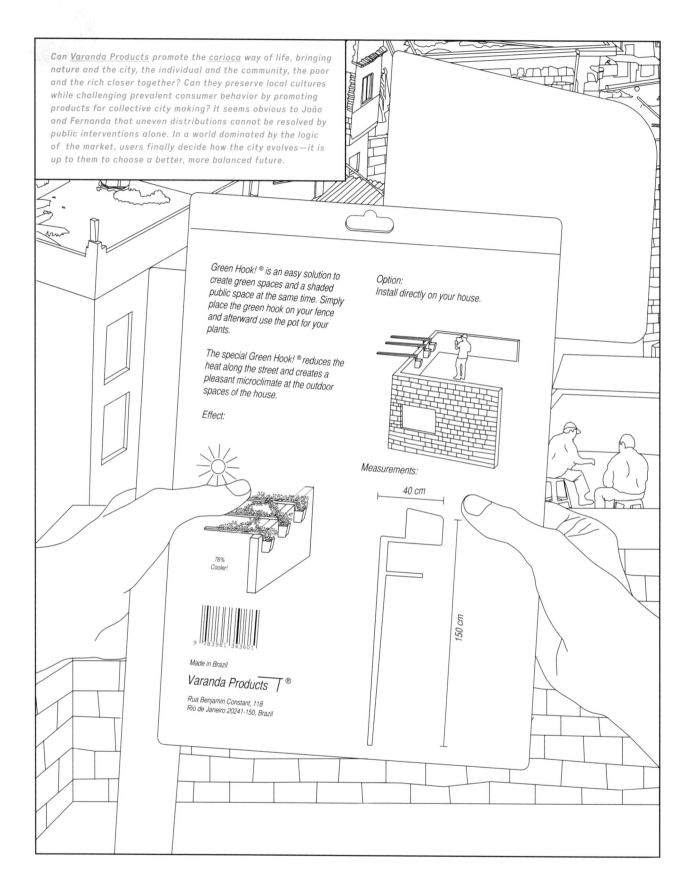

Can *Varanda Products* promote the <u>carioca</u> way of life, bringing nature and the city, the individual and the community, the poor and the rich closer together? Can they preserve local cultures while challenging prevalent consumer behavior by promoting products for collective city making? It seems obvious to João and Fernanda that uneven distributions cannot be resolved by public interventions alone. In a world dominated by the logic of the market, users finally decide how the city evolves—it is up to them to choose a better, more balanced future.

Green Hook! ® is an easy solution to create green spaces and a shaded public space at the same time. Simply place the green hook on your fence and afterward use the pot for your plants.

The special Green Hook! ® reduces the heat along the street and creates a pleasant microclimate at the outdoor spaces of the house.

Effect:

76%
Cooler!

Option:
Install directly on your house.

Measurements:

40 cm

150 cm

Made in Brazil

Varanda Products ⊤ ®

Rua Benjamin Constant, 118
Rio de Janeiro 20241-150, Brazil

RUA Arquitetos & MAS Urban Design, ETH Zurich

TACTICAL URBANISMS: LATIN AMERICA

Todo Por la Praxis with Grupo de Investigación en Arte y Entorno (GIAI AE). "La pregonera," Santiago Tepalcatlpan, Xochimilco. 2013

"Eu Quero Nadar no Capibaribe. E você?" with Bureau A and FORMI. Praias do Capibaribe, Recife, Brazil. 2014

Basurama. RUS Lima, temporary amusement park, Lima. 2010. CC-BY-NA 3.0

Ciudad Emergente. Recycling plaza, Valparaiso. 2013

PKMN (pacman) Architectures and Estudiantes de arquitectura del Instituto Tecnológico de Chihuahua II. Tirando la onda a la escala 1:1, Chihuahua. 2010

a77 + CoZA + Maquila in CheLA. El Gran Aula, Festival Sobre Ruedas, Parque de los Patricios, C.A.B.A., Argentina. 2013

Lucia Monge. Plantón Móvil, Noche en Blanco, Lima. 2012

Universidad de Ingeniería y Tecnología (UTEC). Water Harvesting Billboard on the Pan-American Highway, Lima desert, Peru. 2013

Torre David, Caracas. 2011

DOBRA Oficina de Arquitetura & Paula Bruzzi. Museu do Instante, Belo Horizonte. 2014

Héctor Zamora. *Paracaidista Av. Revolución 1608 bis*, Mexico City. 2004

Micrópolis. Quintal Eletronika, Belo Horizonte. 2012

Carlos M Teixeira and Louise Ganz of Vazio S/A. Topographical Amnesias II, Belo Horizonte. 2004

For more information:
http://unevengrowth.moma.org

Project Credits

Hong Kong

MAP Office

Based in Hong Kong since 1995, MAP Office is a multidisciplinary platform devised by Laurent Gutierrez and Valérie Portefaix that works on physical and imaginary territories using a variety of media to critique spatio-temporal anomalies. Both teach at the School of Design, Polytechnic University. www.map-office.com

Project Directors: Laurent Gutierrez and Valérie Portefaix

Project Supervisor (Cartography): Gilles Vanderstocken

Project Manager: Henry Temple

Project Assistants (Cartography): Jenny Choi Hoi Ki, Xavier Chow Wai Yin, Hugo Huang Jiawu, Venus Lung Yin Fei, Winson Man Ting Fung, Tammy Tang Chi Ching, and Vivienne Yang Jiawei

Network Architecture Lab

The Network Architecture Lab is an experimental unit at the Columbia University Graduate School of Architecture, Planning, and Preservation, established in 2006 by Kazys Varnelis. The Netlab investigates the impacts of digital technology, telecommunications, and changing sociocultural conditions on architecture, the city, and society. www.networkarchitecturelab.org

Director and Editor, *New City Reader*: Kazys Varnelis

Game Design, Symtactics: Jochen Hartmann

Graphic Design, *New City Reader*: Neil Donnelly

Design and Managing Editor, *New City Reader*: Brigette Borders

Editor, *New City Reader*: Robert Sumrell

Project Funding and Support: Design Trust, Hong Kong Ambassadors of Design; Urban Environments Lab, School of Design, The Hong Kong Polytechnic University; Graduate School of Architecture, Planning, and Preservation, Columbia University

Istanbul

Superpool

Superpool, founded by Selva Gürdoğan and Gregers Tang Thomsen in 2006, critically investigates Istanbul through exhibitions and temporary projects including *Mapping Istanbul* (Garanti Gallery/SALT, 2009), a two-year project examining the city through maps, comparative research, and essays. www.superpool.org

Nikitas Gkavogiannis, Selva Gürdoğan, Gregers Tang Thomsen, Zehra Nur Eliaçık, Derya İyikul, and

Betül Nuhoğlu, in collaboration with Memed Erdener, Asbjørn Lund, and Fahri Özkaramanlı

Vienna MAK Workshop Participants: Matthieu Floret, Zoe Georgiou, Christiane Hütter, and May Krivanish

Shenzhen Workshop Participants: Chu Hou San and Tiago Guilherme Cheong

Atelier d'Architecture Autogérée

Founded by Constantin Petcou and Doina Petrescu in 2001, Atelier d'Architecture Autogérée conducts actions and research on participative architecture, developing tools to enable collective appropriation of temporarily available spaces by city dwellers and their transformation into self-managed urban commons. www.urbantactics.org/

Constantin Petcou and Doina Petrescu, in collaboration with Marguerite Wable, Jeremy Galvan, Beste Kuşçu, Augustin Reynaud, and Kim Trogal

We would like to thank Andreas Lang (Public Works) and Kathrin Böhm (myvillages.org) for their advice and long-term collaboration.

Lagos

NLÉ

NLÉ is an architecture, design, and urbanism practice based in Lagos and Amsterdam focusing on city development research and strategy advisory service; conceptualization and creative structuring; architecture, products, and infrastructure design; and arts and cultural urban interventions. www.nleworks.com

Uneven Growth Team: Kunlé Adeyemi, Farooq Adenugba, Marco Cestarolli, Berend Strijland, and Olina Terzi

Collaborators: Tunji Badejo, Olalekan Jeyifous, and QCP Television

Zoohaus/Inteligencias Colectivas
Inteligencias Colectivas is an open free database of nonstandard architectural and urban solutions developed by Zoohaus. Zoohaus is an ever-evolving meta-studio of individuals and collectives working together from different parts of the world. www.inteligenciascolectivas.org

Uneven Growth Team: David Berkvens, Juan Chacón, Manuel Domínguez, Maé Durant, Esteban Fuertes, Luis Galán, Elisa de los Reyes García, Juanito Jones, Manuel Pascual, Luis de Prada, and Lys Villalba, with the contributions of Alfredo Borghi, Miguel Martinez, Daniel Morcillo, Julia García, Aintzane del Río, and Monk Jones

Zoohaus could not have developed this project without the support of the AECID (Spanish Agency for International Development Cooperation); the Spanish Embassy in Abuja; Ministerio de Educación, Cultura y Deporte—Gobierno de España; Acción Cultural Española (AC/E); and Spain Culture New York.

Zoohaus would like to thank the Una Más Una team; New Yorkers Ana Peñalba and David Peña, Andrés Jaque and the Urban Enactments Studio, Michael Sorkin, and Chus

Martínez; Lagosians Mr. Ayo Ola, Nike, Laura Fortes, and Captain As Dahiru and all the Air Force Military base crew; Guillaume Monfort; Wiener Pablo Román; Flickr CC Warriors Satanoid, Ben Freeman, and Stefan Magdalinski; and professor and friend Izaskun Chinchilla.

NLÉ and Zoohaus would like to thank Pedro Gadanho and the MoMA and MAK crew; the Shenzhen Biennale workshop participants Qing Ye, Wei Han, Nestor San Valentin, and Xiaowei Zhuang; and the Vienna MAK workshop participants Anna Ohlmeier, Ehsan Bazafkan, Marlene Wagner, Leila Bochicchio, and Hsiang Max.

Mumbai

URBZ: user-generated cities
URBZ, founded by Matias Echanove, Rahul Srivastava, and Geeta Mehta in 2008, learns from its environment while contributing to its improvement. With offices in Mumbai and Goa, URBZ organizes participatory planning and design workshops in multiple countries. http://urbz.net/

Founding Partners: Matias Echanove, Rahul Srivastava, and Geeta Mehta

Uneven Growth Team: Matias Echanove, Rahul Srivastava, Yehuda Safran, Ishan Tankha, Sameep Padora, Diane Athaide, Ismini Christakopoulou, Jai Bhadgaonkar, Bharat Gangurde, Shyam Kanle, Aki Lee, Itai Margula, Shardul Patil, and Aditi Nair

Ensamble Studio/MIT-POPlab
Antón García-Abril and Débora Mesa, principals of the multidisciplinary Ensamble Studio, founded POPlab (Prototypes of Prefabrication Laboratory) at the Massachusetts

Workshop, MoMA PS1. October 2013

Institute of Technology (MIT) in 2013 as a research laboratory bridging the gaps between architecture, science, urban design, infrastructure, and people. www.ensamble.info; poplab.mit.edu

Ensamble Studio Principals and Founders of POPlab at MIT: Antón García-Abril, and Débora Mesa

Ensamble Studio/POPlab Team: Antón García-Abril, Débora Mesa, Javier Cuesta, Ricardo Sanz, Marie Benaboud, Simone Cavallo, José María Lavena, Massimo Loia, Borja Soriano, and Erin Soygenis

New York

SITU Studio
Founded in 2005 in Brooklyn, SITU's workspace is split evenly between a fabrication shop and a design studio, reflecting its commitment to interrogating design ideas through physical and material experimentation at a wide range of scales. www.situstudio.com

SITU Studio Principals: Basar Girit, Aleksey Lukyanov-Cherny, Westley Rozen, and Bradley Samuels

Project Manager: McKenna Cole

Team Members: Jennie Bernstein,

Zoe Demple, Kristine Ericson, Hayrettin Gunc, Derek Lange, Gabriel Munnich, Charles-Antoine Perrault, Nina Phinouwong, Katie Shima, and Xiaowei Wang

Consultants: Jesse M. Keenan, Center for Urban Real Estate (CURE.), Columbia University; Michael Amabile, Arup; Sarah Watson, Citizens Housing Planning Council; Seema Agnani and Drew Goldsman, Chhaya Community Development Corporation; David Giles, Center for an Urban Future; Kevin Findlan, NYU Furman Center; Alex Washburn, Center for Coastal Resilience and Urban Xcellence (CRUX) at Stevens Institute of Technology; John Szot, Brooklyn Digital Foundry; Minkwon Center for Community Action; and MFY Legal Services

Cohabitation Strategies (CohStra)

CohStra is a nonprofit cooperative for socio-spatial research, design, and development founded in the wake of the 2008 financial crash by Lucia Babina, Emiliano Gandolfi, Gabriela Rendón, and Miguel Robles-Durán and based in New York City, Rotterdam, and Ibiza. www.cohstra.org

Founding Members: Lucia Babina, Emiliano Gandolfi, Gabriela Rendón, and Miguel Robles-Durán

Uneven Growth Team: Raquel de Anda, curator; Guillermo Delgado, urbanist; Juan Junca, urban planner; Jonathan Lapalme, urban strategist; Phillip Lühl, architect; Juan Pemberty, design thinker; Santiago Giraldo, urban ecologist; and Rajesh Bhavnani, animation director

We would like to thank for their advice Tom Angotti, Professor of Urban Affairs and Planning at Hunter College and the Graduate Center

of CUNY; David Harvey, Distinguished Professor of Anthropology and Geography at the Graduate Center of CUNY; Rachel LaForest, Executive Director of The Right to the City Alliance; and all the people who were instrumental in our work.

Rio de Janeiro

RUA Arquitetos

Rua is the word for "street" in Portuguese. Founded by Pedro Évora and Pedro Rivera in 2008, RUA Arquitetos is interested in how architecture can mediate and promote space for social exchange through projects in the informal areas of Rio de Janeiro. www.rualab.com

Coordinators: Pedro Évora and Pedro Rivera

Collaborators: Aliki Kostopoulou, Fabiano Pires, Natalia Winnika, Mariana Albuquerque, Mariana Meneguetti, and Roberto Costa

MAS Urban Design, ETH Zurich

MAS Urban Design, chaired by Professor Marc Angélil, is a research and design laboratory that prepares participants for an active role within the interdisciplinary agenda of city planning. Since 2010, classes have investigated new models of urban development for Brazil. www.angelil. arch.ethz.ch

MAS Urban Design Program Chair: Marc Angélil

Coordinators: Marc Angélil, Rainer Hehl, Julian Schubert, Elena Schütz, and Leonard Streich

Students: Yevgeniya Bevz, Andreas Boden, Mengxing Cao, Ondrej Chybík, Andrea de Guio, Marija Gramc

Milivojevic, Heechul Jung, Minami Nagao, Theodora Papamichail, Georgios Papoulias, Artemis Pefani, Theodoros Poulakos, Konstantinos Stoforos, Henrik Syversten, Maria Fernanda Tellez Velasco, Alexander Daxböck, Zoi Georgiou, Gianmaria Socci, Fani Kostourou, Natalia Michailidou, Gerhard Ungersböck Collaborators: João Salsa, Filipe Serro, and Tobias Müller

Workshop, Shenzhen—Hong Kong Bi-City Biennale of Urbanism and Architecture. December 2013

Workshop, MAK—Austrian Museum of Applied Arts / Contemporary Art, Vienna. June 2014

Illustration Credits

In reproducing the images contained in this publication, the Museum obtained the permission of the rights holders whenever possible. In those instances where the Museum could not locate the rights holders, notwithstanding good-faith efforts, it requests that any contact information concerning such rights holders be forwarded so that they may be contacted for future editions.

Ahmed Abd El-Fatah: 49 (bottom right); Jeyhoun Allebaugh: 135 (right); AP Photo/ Felipe Dana: 27 (top); © Archigram 1964, photo: Department of Imaging Services, The Museum of Modern Art: 22; Architecture and Vision: 30 (bottom); © Yann Arthus-Bertrand: 99; © 2014 Artists Rights Society (ARS), New York/ ADAGP, Paris/FLC: 34 (bottom); Atelier d'Architecture Autogérée: 83, 84 (except second row middle), 85–93; Atelier OPA Co., Ltd.: 19; Iwan Baan: 16, 18, 21, 108 (bottom left); © 2014 Evan Browning: 42, 43 (bottom); © ChantalS – Fotolia: 49 (top left); Yasuyoshi Chiba/AFP/ Getty Images: 17; Ismini Christakopoulou: 120 (bottom), 121; Dirk Coetser/Architecture for a Change: 27 (bottom); CohStra: 133–34, 136, 138–39, 142 (left); Laszlo Csutoras: 31; Rick Darke: 60 (bottom); Photo: Department of Imaging Services, The Museum of Modern Art: 59 (top), 131 (left); Mark Joel V. Dyoco: 44 (bottom); Matias Echanove: 117; Eko Atlantic: 103 (fourth row right); Greg Elsner: 53 (top); Ensamble Studio/ MIT-POPlab: 122–27; © Marc Ericson: 57; Estudio Teddy Cruz: 51 (top), 52 (top), 53 (bottom), 54, 55; William Farrington/Polaris Images: 131 (right); Pedro Gadanho: 164 (bottom); Jorge Gamboa: 63; The Getty Research Institute, Los Angeles (P850002 (37)): 38; Christoph Gielen: "Ciphers," courtesy Jovis Verlag, Berlin: 50; Alf Gillman at http://www.flickr.com/photos/alfgillman: 110 (bottom left); Adela Goldbard: 51 (bottom); © 2014 David Goldblatt: 34 (top); Julien Gregorio: 118 (top right); GUST Photography/courtesy Kohn Pedersen Fox Associates: 37; Luke James Hayes & AFFECT-T: 29; Lewis Jones: 23 (bottom); David Jurca: 52 (bottom); Russ Juskalian: 59; © 2014 Hilary Koob-Sassen: 41 (right), 47; Lagos Metropolitan Area Transport Authority (LAMATA): 103 (third row left); Aki Lee: 115; © 2014 Sze Tsung Leong, photo: Department of Imaging Services, The Museum of Modern Art: 15; John Locke: 61 (bottom); © 2014 Rut Blees Luxemburg: 44 (top), 45; Pablo López Luz: 33; © Danny Lyon/Magnum Photos: 35; Doug Mahugh: 58; Photograph © MAK/Mika K. Wisskirchen: 164 (top); Oleksandr Maksymenko: 28; MAP Office: 67–77; The Network Architecture Lab: 78–79; Neville Mars: 49 (top right); © Adrian Melis: 60 (top); © 2014 Melissa Moore: 41 (left), 46; New York City Department of Buildings: 132; NLÉ and Zoohaus/Inteligencias Colectivas: 101 (top), 102–3 (except those © QCPTV, below); Cyril Nottelet and Al Borde: 39; Olabode Olaleye: 106 (bottom left); Diekola

Onaolapo: 110 (top left); Yuzuri Onoue: 25; © QCPTV: 100, 101 (bottom), 102 (first row middle, second row right, third row right), 103 (first row right, second row left), 108 (top left); Jonathan Rashad: 62; REUTERS/Stringer: 30 (top); Pedro Rivera: 147; Julie Roth: 43 (top); RUA Arquitetos and MAS Urban Design, ETH Zurich: 148–59; SITU Studio: 135 (left), 137, 140–41, 142 (right), 143; SOM/Nick Merrick © Hedrich Blessing: 49 (bottom left); © Edmund Sumner/VIEWpictures.co.uk: 61 (top); Superpool: 84 (second row middle), 94–95; Superstudio, © 1971 Archivio Superstudio, photo: Department of Imaging Services, The Museum of Modern Art: 23 (top); Ishan Tankha: 116, 118 (bottom left and right), 120; Serkan Taycan: 36 (top); Andrew P. Tucker: 163; TYIN tegnestue Architects: 36 (bottom); URBZ: 119, 120 (middle); © URBZOO: 24; © Michael Wolf, courtesy the artist and Bruce Silverstein Gallery, New York: 20

Illustration Credits, Tactical Urbanisms

Page 80 (clockwise from top left): thecaveworkshop; The Museum of Modern Art, New York, © 2014 Didier Faustino; Glenn Eugen Ellingsen; ENCORE HEUREUX + G.studio; Sierra Forest; Shinkenchiku-sha; standardarchitecture. Page 81 (clockwise from top left): John Lin and Olivier Ottevaere; Fang Zhenning; Voluntary Architects' Network; Masaki Koizumi; Marco Casagrande; CL3 and West Kowloon Cultural District Authority; © West 8 urban design & landscape architecture. Page 96 (clockwise from top left): Studio Karl Philips; Maria Papadimitriou; Aris Kamarotos; Marcos Domingo; Stefano Mont Girbés; Ragnhild Lübbert Terpling; NL Architects. Page 97 (clockwise from top left): Photograph © Laurent Garbit/Malka Architecture 2013; Dosfotos; StiftungFREIZEIT; Recetas Urbanas; Oliver Schau; Ben Pohl/UD; Vittoria Martini, © Thomas Hirschhorn, courtesy the artist and Gladstone Gallery, New York and Brussels. Page 112 (clockwise from top left): Hamish Appleby; Tomás Munita for the *New York Times*; Robert Eke; Mauro Pinto; Matteo Ferroni; Heath Nash. Page 113 (clockwise from top left): Moladi; r1; Sumbu Chantraine Temo; Peter Rich Architects; Nic Bothma; Machiel Erasmus; Amanda McCaulley. Page 128 (clockwise from top left): Akshay Sharma; Abin Chaudhuri; Bakul Foundation; Meena Kadri; George Friedman, © Kohler Co. 2014. Page 129 (clockwise from top left): CRIT, Mumbai; Felipe Vera, Urban South Asia Project at Harvard Graduate School of Design; SABA; Filipe Balestra & Sara Göransson/ Urban Nouveau; Cynthia Koenig/Wello; Urfunlab Surat. Page 144 (clockwise from top left): Eric Rosewall, Depave; Anne Hamersky; Antonia Belt; Michael Rakowitz, courtesy the artist and Lombard Freid Gallery, New York; Mark Reigelman II; Michael Falco. Page 145 (clockwise from top

left): NYC DOT; Eymund Diegel; Marcos Zotes; Timothy Hursley; Rebar Group/Andrea Scher; San Francisco Planning Department, Pavement to Parks Program; Keith Hartwig; photograph © Jonathan Traveisa, 2012. Page 160 (clockwise from top left): Grupo de Investigación en Arte y Entorno (GIAI AE); Basurama.org CC-BY-NA 3.0; Fundação Joaquim Nabuco (FUNDAJ); PKMN (pacman) Architectures; M. Mercedes Sánchez; Bárbara Barreda of Ciudad Emergente. Page 161 (clockwise from top left): Josip Curich; Diego Santillan Navarro; Iwan Baan; Fernando Medellin, © Héctor Zamora, courtesy the artist and Luciana Brito and Labor galleries; Eduardo Eckenfels; Mateus Lira; Rosanna Rüttinger

Acknowledgments

Given the conceptual breadth and broad geographic territory *Uneven Growth* draws on, the exhibition and catalogue have necessarily been the work of a several institutions and a large number of individuals. First and foremost, the project was made possible by a generous collaboration with the MAK - Austrian Museum of Applied Arts / Contemporary Art, Vienna, which will provide a second venue for the exhibition. We are grateful to Christoph Thun-Hohenstein, Director; Simon Rees, former Head of Programming and Development; Bärbel Vischer, Curator of Contemporary Art; and their MAK colleagues for their encouragement and commitment.

Over the course of its fourteen-month initiative, *Uneven Growth* has benefited from advice and commentary by a group of outside scholars, designers, and critics. During the first project phase in New York, a team of advisers provided early feedback: Nader Tehrani, Professor and Head of the Department of Architecture at MIT; Michael Sorkin, Principal of Michael Sorkin Studio; Alfredo Brillembourg, Founding Partner of Urban-Think Tank; Mimi Zeiger, *Loud Paper*; Saskia Sassen, Robert S. Lynd Professor of Sociology at Columbia University; Teddy Cruz, Associate Professor at University of California, San Diego; Diana Balmori, Balmori Associates; Neil Brenner, Professor of Urban Theory and Director of the Urban Theory Lab at the Graduate School of Design,

Harvard University; Ken Farmer, Project for Public Spaces; Cathy Lang Ho, editor and curator; Ed Keller and Carla Leitão, AUM Studio; Harvey Molotch, Professor of Sociology and Metropolitan Studies at New York University; Quilian Riano, DSGN AGNC; and Damon Rich, Planning Director and Chief Urban Designer for the City of Newark, New Jersey. At the Shenzhen Bi-City Biennale of Urbanism/Architecture, Ole Bouman, Creative Director, and Vivian Zuidhof, Project Coordinator, were gracious hosts to a second workshop and intermediate exhibition display. At this time, besides the participation of dedicated local students, who both worked with teams and recorded the event, scholars and architects based in Shenzhen, Hong Kong, Macao, and elsewhere have also offered their generous insights and critiques, namely Ying Jiang, O-office Architects; Eric Schuldenfrei and Marisa Yiu, ESKYIU Architecture; Doreen Liu and Thomas Ching, Chinese University of Hong Kong; Juan Du, Department of Architecture, University of Hong Kong; Diogo Teixeira, University of Saint Joseph; Tao Chen, architect; and Arjen Oosterman and Lilet Breddels, *Archis* magazine. At the final workshop hosted by MAK Vienna, we enjoyed discerning presentations by Alice Rawsthorn, the *New York Times*, London; Elke Krasny, Senior Lecturer at the Academy of Fine Arts, Vienna; Hani Rashid, Asymptote Architecture, New York; and Ricky

Burdett, Professor of Urban Studies at the London School of Economics and Political Science, London. Again, students from an international range offered an invaluable contribution to the workshops, and Vienna-based architects and scholars provided insightful responses to the teams' interim presentations, namely Dietmar Steiner, Architekturzentrum Wien; Stefan Gruber, Academy of Fine Arts Vienna; Anton Falkeis, University of Applied Arts Vienna; Andreas Rumpfhuber, Expanded Design; Christine Schwaiger, New Design University, St. Pölten; Michael Rieper, MVD Austria; and Helge Mooshammer, Vienna University of Technology

At The Museum of Modern Art, we are grateful to the leadership and counsel of Glenn D. Lowry, Director; Ramona Bannayan, Senior Deputy Director for Exhibitions, Collections, and Programs; Todd Bishop, Senior Deputy Director, External Affairs; James Gara, Chief Operating Officer; Peter Reed, Senior Deputy Director for Curatorial Affairs; and Trish Jeffers, Director of Human Resources. Our colleagues at MoMA PS1 were instrumental in the early stages of the project; we extend thanks to Klaus Biesenbach, Director, and Jenny Schlenzka, Assistant Curator, for their crucial support.

Generous support by our sponsors has been integral to the realization of this project. Foremost thanks go to Andre Singer, for his major support to the exhibition, the third he has supported in the series Issues in Contemporary Architecture. We express sincere thanks to MoMA's Wallis Annenberg Fund for Innovation in Contemporary Art through the Annenberg Foundation for their support to the exhibition and the workshop at MoMA PS1. For helping to fund this publication, we deeply appreciate the support of the Dale S. and Norman Mills Leff Publication Fund.

In the Department of Development, we are grateful to Lauren Stakias, Director, Exhibition and Program Funding; Sylvia Renner, Senior Development Officer, International Funding; Claire Huddleston, Development Officer; and Kayla Rakowski, Development Officer. We thank the Departments of Marketing and Communications for ensuring the exhibition's public presence: Kim Mitchell, Chief Communications Officer; Margaret Doyle, Director of Communications; Meg Montgoris, Publicist; Rebecca Stokes, Director of Digital Marketing; Jason Persse, Manager; Carolyn Kelly, Coordinating Editor; and Victor Samra, Digital Media Marketing Manager.

In an exhibition that spans six cities and encompasses work by a diverse set of architects, we are grateful to the Departments of Graphic Design and Exhibition Design and Production for finding creative ways to articulate and skillfully produce the design proposals. We extend our appreciation to Mack Cole-Edelsack, Exhibition Designer, who oversaw the installation; to Allan Smith, Foreman, with his team in the Carpenter Shop, and to Bryan Reyna, with his team of painters. In the Department of Graphic Design, we value the exceptional work of Ingrid Chou, Associate Creative Director; Sabine Dowek, Art Director; Claire Corey, Production Manager; and Pei-Y Ni, Graphic Designer. A superb A/V team lent their expertise and inventive solutions to the exhibition's multimedia: Aaron Louis, A/V Director; Aaron Harrow, Design Manager; Mike Gibbons, A/V Technician; and Peter Oleksik, Assistant Media Conservator, Department of Conservation. In Digital Media, we extend thanks to Shannon Darrough, Director; Maggie Lederer, Senior Producer; Nina Callaway; and Han Li. In concert with the work of Digital Media, we are grateful to Arch & Loop, who crafted a bold online space to represent the exhibition and collect public image submissions; we thank Lydia Turner, Martin Zagorsek, Sean Conway, and Francesca Campanella.

In the Department of Exhibitions, we express sincere thanks to Erik Patton, Associate Director, and Rachel Kim, Assistant Coordinator. Nancy Adelson, Deputy General Counsel; Alexis Sandler, Associate General Counsel; and Dina Sorokina, Department Manager and Paralegal, have provided advice on all legal matters. In coordinating the exhibition's checklist, we are grateful to the Department of Collection Management and Exhibition Registration: Caitlin Kelly, Senior Registrar Assistant; Ian Eckert, Manager; Kat Ryan, Coordinator; and Leslie Ornstein, Assistant. Our colleagues Tunji Adeniji, Director of Facilities and Safety; LJ Hartman, Director of Security; Rob Jung, Manager; and Sarah Wood, Assistant Manager, have been indispensable to the management of operations, in-house transportation, installation, and security.

In the Department of Education, we appreciate the support of Wendy Woon, The Edward John Noble Foundation Deputy Director of Education; Pablo Helguera, Director, Adult and Academic Education; and Sara Bodinson, Director, Interpretation and Research, in organizing the exhibition's public programs and making the project accessible to a wider public.

In the Department of Architecture and Design, we enjoyed support and encouragement from the entire staff. We extend special thanks to Barry Bergdoll, Curator, Department of Architecture and Design, for contributing the preface to this volume and providing valuable feedback throughout the project; Emma Presler, Department Manager, for sharing her experience and know-how; Phoebe Springstubb, Curatorial Assistant, for her versatile support; Leah Barreras, Department Assistant, for her critical coordination skills; and interns Sarah Rafson, Anna Renken, Melinda Zoephel, Lisa Tannenbaum, and Christopher Ball for their tactical urbanism research and careful work on the catalogue's image permissions.

The success of this catalogue is indebted to the Department of Publications. We thank: Christopher Hudson, Publisher; Chul R. Kim, Associate Publisher; David Frankel, Editorial Director; Marc Sapir, Production Director; and Makiko Wholey, Department Coordinator. We are especially grateful to editor Ron Broadhurst, whose nimble editorial work bridged disciplines, and to Hannah Kim, Production Coordinator, who kept us on track. The deft design work and perceptive layout by Adam Michaels and Anna Rieger of Project Projects brings the book together. And finally, this project would not have been possible without the efforts of the twelve architecture practices who came together from around the world, dedicating their time and innovative thinking in the spirit of positive change.

—Pedro Gadanho
Curator, Department of Architecture and Design, The Museum of Modern Art